THE RESCUE
AT DEAD DOG BEACH

One Man's Quest
to Find a Home for the
World's Forgotten Animals

itbooks

AN IMPRINT OF HARPERCOLLINS PUBLISHERS

THE RESCUE AT DEAD DOG BEACH

Stephen McGarva

THE RESCUE AT DEAD DOG BEACH. Copyright © 2014 by Stephen McGarva. All rights reserved. Printed in the United States of America. No part of this book may be used or reproduced in any manner whatsoever without written permission except in the case of brief quotations embodied in critical articles and reviews. For information address HarperCollins Publishers, 195 Broadway, New York, New York 10007.

HarperCollins books may be purchased for educational, business, or sales promotional use. For information please e-mail the Special Markets Department at SPsales@harpercollins.com.

FIRST EDITION

Designed by Shannon Plunkett

Library of Congress Cataloging-in-Publication Data has been applied for.

ISBN 978-0-06-201408-5

14 15 16 17 18   OV/RRD   10 9 8 7 6 5 4 3 2 1

This is a work of nonfiction. The events and experiences detailed herein are all true and have been faithfully rendered as I have remembered them, to the best of my ability. Some names, identities, and circumstances have been changed in order to protect the integrity and/or anonymity of the various individuals involved. Though conversations come from my keen recollection of them, they are not written to represent word-for-word documentation; rather, I've retold them in a way that evokes the real feeling and meaning of what was said, in keeping with the true essence of the mood and spirit of the event.

To my beloved German shepherd Achates, and to the many teachers that passed through my life at Dead Dog Beach. You shared your wisdom without words. You were my friends, therapists, and protectors. You gave meaning to my life when I was lost, and left a legacy beyond words. You will always be loved and never be forgotten.

The dog is a gentleman;
I hope to go to his heaven, not man's.

—Mark Twain, letter to W. D. Howells,
April 2, 1899

Millions of families in America have pet dogs. Many books have been written about those relationships. Sadly, there are far more dogs in the world that aren't lucky enough to have human families. This book is about those dogs.

People who travel around the world are often greeted by a heart-wrenching sight: dogs or cats starving and sick in the street, shooed away from restaurants by waiters, and ignored by almost everyone else. It is usually only when one of these dogs bites or infects a human being that a community decides to do something about it, and then a lot of innocent living beings are rounded up and slaughtered.

What I describe in the following pages about my two years in Puerto Rico can be tough going at times. What a few bad, or simply thoughtless, people did to dogs on the island, in particular at Playa Lucia, or what's aptly known as Dead Dog Beach, is hard to fathom. If I hadn't witnessed the cruelty firsthand, day after day, I wouldn't have believed human beings could be so heartless and cruel to other living creatures.

It's important to consider the context in which the events that I describe in this book occurred. Despite its idyllic location in the sunny Caribbean, Puerto Rico suffers from a poor economy, high government debt that has led to austerity measures and reduced services, and a spectacularly high crime rate. According to CNN, there were somewhere north of sixty-eight thousand violent crimes reported in 2008, an increase of 9.3 percent from the previous year, this among a population of less than four million (and shrinking annually thanks to emigration to the mainland). In early 2013, *Morning Edition* on National Public Radio ran a four-part series called "Puerto Rico: A Disenchanted Island," which discussed "how Puerto Rico's troubles," including a "deteriorating economy, increased poverty, and a swelling crime rate," were affecting the island's population. An article in the *New York Times* on June, 21, 2011, titled "Murder Rate and Fear Rise in Puerto Rico," noted that while homicides were most prevalent in poor areas, they "occasionally spilled into San Juan's tourist areas and crossed into wealthy districts." Compounding the drug-trafficking–fueled violence, the police department has itself been subject to investigation by the U.S. Justice Department, and the American Civil Liberties Union "has compiled its own report listing accusations of abuse by police officers against Puerto Ricans."

In no way do I mean to condemn all of Puerto Rico or its residents. It is a spectacularly beautiful island populated by many warmhearted people. I also want to make clear that what happened to the dogs was at the hands of a particular group of people. Indeed, if I had not stumbled onto *that* beach and found *that* group of dogs, I would have had an amazing few years living on this tropical island. But, the truth is, I did find that beach and those dogs, and my life was forever changed.

If the scenes I describe here are difficult to read about, it is important that you don't turn away. We must bear witness to what happened on Dead Dog Beach, and what is still happening there and around the world. Please keep reading and spread the word.

THE RESCUE AT DEAD DOG BEACH

T he day began like any other: I was doing my morning rounds with the dogs, as I had been for more than a year now. I parked my SUV by the large metal shipping containers at the entrance to the beach and walked the dirt road down to the water, looking for newly dumped dogs. They usually arrived scared, hungry, and badly abused. Those were the lucky ones. I also scanned for the remains of those who'd died in the night, often of gunshot or machete wounds if not from simple neglect and starvation. The air was filled with the singing of the coquis, the tiny native frogs who lived in the trash piled among the palm trees.

The lush vegetation that lined the road often reeked of decay. When I arrived at the water's edge to begin my first feeding, the dogs—my pack—gathered around like they always did. They were eager but orderly, in antic-ipation of food and human kindness. The hairless leather skin, the visible festering wounds on their bodies, the disfigurement of mange and broken bones—none of these horrible afflictions masked the dogs' inherent sweet-ness and desire for basic affection.

Suddenly the pack ran a few yards down the beach, excited by something.

I looked up and, not far from where I was feeding the dogs, there was a young horse lying quartered and decapitated, ropes still tied to its legs and head. From the tire tracks in the sand, I could tell that it had been ripped apart by pickup trucks. Dogs weren't the only animals that suffered in this tropical paradise. Any animal that had outlived its usefulness, even if solely due to a lack of proper care by its human owners, could end up at this remote beach, far from public scrutiny, as a victim.

The horse looked like it had been blown open, its blood, sinews, and viscera scattered across the white sand.

Through the cloud of swarming flies, I saw movement inside the obliterated torso. A small puppy lazily stretched out its legs amid the entrails. It had crawled inside the dead horse to fend off the morning chill.

I reached into the mare's carcass and grabbed the puppy. She wiggled and squeaked as she looked up into my eyes, surprised to see me. A sickly-sweet blood and horse smell wafted off of her. She yawned and nosed my damp hand.

I carried her to the water to wash off the gore, then dried her with my shirt and cradled her to my body as I walked back up the dirt road to my truck. The pack followed me, their tails wagging in anticipation of breakfast.

In the tall grass to the right of the road, I heard a squeak followed by a muffled moan. Still cradling the puppy in my arms, I pushed the grass aside with my foot. Three more puppies, the rest of this one's litter, were suckling on their dead mother. She had a foamy film around her mouth, the telltale sign of poisoning, another common method for eliminating unwanted dogs.

And so began another day at Playa Lucia—a tropical paradise I came to know as Dead Dog Beach.

ONE

When I was a kid, I ran away from home every time one of our pets died. Dogs, cats, birds, gerbils, hamsters: if it died, I was gone. I couldn't comprehend that people and pets I loved just switched off, despite how I felt about them. I wanted to feel more powerful than death. But instead I was helpless before it, so I ran. Death terrified me.

My dad, who had suffered from severe alcoholism, died a month after my eleventh birthday. I ran for miles and miles that day, then lay down in the tall grass of the countryside where I lived, until it got dark. My family worried each time I bolted, but they knew my routine. If they chased me, I'd go farther. So they quietly waited. They knew I'd be back once the pain eased.

After my dad's death, I struggled with myself and just about everyone else. I used to be a friendly, sociable kid, but now I got into a lot of fights at school—with classmates and with teachers who made me feel inadequate because I was dyslexic and not a great learner. My mom was always getting called into school because of the trouble I got into, which made me feel guilty for causing her more pain.

To console me and help fill the emptiness, my mother got me a beautiful German shepherd puppy. I named her Tanya, after a friend of mine's hippie older sister who was always very kind to me and who, in retrospect, I probably had a huge crush on. My mother's plan worked. Tanya, the big, lovable German shepherd, and I were soon inseparable.

A few months later—less than a year after losing my dad—my grandpa died. He was the last remaining male adult in my life. After that, I withdrew completely. I mostly spoke to my dog; only when necessary did I speak to my mum, my nan, or my brothers. Soon Tanya was about the only friend I confided in. We slept together every night, my arm around her warm torso, its rising and falling soothing me to sleep.

I confided all my pain, loneliness, and hardest times to Tanya, and she listened patiently—and understood. When the local bully came near, Tanya would raise a lip and growl, and he knew not to touch me. In time, Tanya even drew me out of my shell. She was a very loving dog and seemed to recognize people with good hearts. When we ran around the neighborhood together, dodging in and out of the Russian oaks, she lured good-hearted people back into my life, and soon I was starting to socialize again.

One afternoon I was in the backyard playing with Tanya and a neighbor's dog named Doobie. The two dogs ran full speed side by side and playfully nipped at each other's necks. Suddenly Doobie broke formation, bolting through the partially open gate and across the street. Tanya made as if to follow her companion but stopped in her tracks and looked back at me when I called for her to stop. In my peripheral vision, I caught sight of an exhaust-spewing old pickup truck racing down the street. I heard the din of its rusty muffler. The pursuit instinct and the thrill of the chase won out over obedience. Tanya and the truck were destinies about to collide. Doobie ran free and clear while Tanya was not so lucky. A bleary-eyed driver stepped out of the vehicle smelling of whiskey and cigarettes.

Please. Please. Please. Don't let her die. It's my fault. I did this to her. My thoughts were running into and over one another, tumbling in a bloody confusion of guilt and shame.

Sitting in the bed of the truck, I held her head in my lap, trying to soothe her but barely being able to stomach the agonizing sounds of her whimpering in pain. It was too much to bear. Not a boy but not yet a man, I cried as the truck that put us in this position delivered us to the vet.

I held her close as the vet pushed the needle into her vein. I begged Tanya not to leave me. Not now. I felt her chest gently rise and fall for the last time as she took her final breath.

"Stay as long as you need to, son."

Tanya was gone, and I was alone again. Saying good-bye felt like an eternity. Dogs have to die. Boys have to grieve. Life is not easy. When I summoned enough strength to stand, I wiped the snot and tears off my face, walked out of the office, and started running.

When I couldn't run anymore, I collapsed in the grass and cried until my heart rate and breathing slowed. The moment drifted away, replaced by a numb sadness and the inevitable return of my own powerlessness to change destiny.

After losing my best friend, the symbolic replacement for my father's love, I struggled again.

At fifteen, I felt so much despair that I tried to kill myself. From that point forward, I remained guarded and distant emotionally. I faked happiness so as not to be asked questions or draw attention to myself.

Then I got my act together, and, at age seventeen, I graduated from high school and volunteered to travel to Southeast Asia to work with orphaned children for three years. It was the change of environment and perspective I desperately needed. Seeing innocent children struggle from day to day just to survive made it impossible to keep feeling sorry for myself.

As a result of my attempts to outrun pain, I became an escape artist. I escaped into art, like painting and sculpture, and into extreme sports, like rock and ice climbing, mountaineering, paragliding, kite surfing. These were the things I felt gave me control over death. The art felt eternal, like I was leaving a piece of myself behind for others, and the sports took me as close to the edge as humanly possible without going over. They became a way of life, a way for me to live completely in the moment, temporarily forgetting everything that would otherwise weigh constantly on my mind.

The sports I do are inherently dangerous, and thus viewed by many as selfish. However, no matter how great the risk, the rewards are greater. The better I became at sports, the more risks I took. And so it's always been hard on anyone who loves me to accept this part of my life. It cost me many relationships before I met my wife, Pam. The women I'd dated had tried to change me, to stop me from risking my life for something so seemingly frivolous. But I lived for the feeling of complete freedom, and I had accepted long ago that I'd likely die in pursuit of it. Because even in these pursuits, somewhere in the back of my mind I knew that I really didn't have any power over death. But when I stood on the fine line separating life and death, I could choose to control my fear.

W hat do you think about moving to Puerto Rico for a few years?" Pam asked me one evening in the spring of 2005. Pam worked at a biotech firm that specializes in developing and manufacturing drugs used to treat cancer, diabetes, and other serious diseases. In her own way, she too was working to beat death. Perhaps that's why she put up with me.

Her bosses in the quality compliance division, where she worked as a liaison between the company and regulatory agencies like the FDA, had asked her to take a short-term assignment at their Juncos site in Puerto Rico, which was home to a state-of-the-art facility for biotechnology manufacturing.

Never one to turn down an adventure, my answer was immediate: "When do we leave?"

We'd moved a couple of years earlier to the historic Hill and Harbor community, originally populated by fishing captains, in East Greenwich, Rhode Island, in hopes of putting down roots. We bought an old house that I put a lot of time into restoring, but all too often Pam was away on business trips, and, frankly the sleepy New England lifestyle was killing me. And despite our best efforts at nesting, Pam and I both suffer from an incurable wanderlust. It was one of the things that attracted us to each other in the first place.

In addition, I still hadn't recovered from the loss of our German shepherd, Achates, a few months earlier. He had been my faithful companion for over ten years, and I missed him terribly. At the end of his life, he had been a noble old man in great pain. Sometimes I wondered if we had delayed the decision too long and selfishly kept him alive. He was like a child to us, and Pam and I had always hoped that, when it was his time to go, he'd just go in his sleep. It didn't happen that way.

Putting a dog down is the darkest day of pet ownership, a decision that doesn't come easy and one that you can never feel proud of, or forget. When we returned home that evening from the vet's office, I told Pam that I would never have another dog. But lately, when she was traveling, I'd been lonely. I had no companion other than a bothersome neighbor who kept asking me to repair things in his home for free.

So this opportunity was a stroke of luck for both of us. It didn't hurt that Puerto Rico happened to be an extreme athlete's paradise. The prospect of moving made me feel more alive than I had in years. I couldn't pack up my art supplies and sports gear fast enough, but it took a few months to iron out the logistics, including finishing the restoration of the house so we could sell it.

In the meantime, we took a reconnaissance trip to the island in April. Pam's company assured us we could back out if we didn't like what we found. I had never been to Puerto Rico before and knew little about the island, but upon arriving in San Juan I was surprised to see the pervasive poverty. While there are plenty of beautiful tourist attractions in the old city—blue cobblestone streets and imposing fortifications dating back to the sixteenth century when the island was a Spanish possession—modern San Juan was a vast sprawl of high-rises amid low-slung cinder-block buildings topped by corrugated metal roofs, all of it enshrouded by dense jungle.

After exploring the city, we drove southeast from San Juan toward the area where we'd be living. The trip was hair-raising, but not just because the local custom for highway driving seemed to have been inspired more by NASCAR than the comparatively polite rules of the road I grew up with.

What really affected us was seeing emaciated dogs wandering the roads, and gaunt horses tied to the freeway guardrails. The animals barely reacted to the cars and trucks whizzing by at seventy miles an hour, less than five feet from them. Every so often we'd see a dog lying prone and lifeless by the side of the road. On one stretch, I saw a horse lying halfway across the slow lane of the freeway. Its legs were akimbo and its head was jammed up against the railing. Rigor mortis had set in. Pam didn't notice, so I chose not to point it out to her.

Finally we crested a hill and caught a glimpse of the Caribbean Sea, twinkling blue out to the horizon. This was more like the paradise we'd both envisioned when Pam got the offer to come here.

Our destination was Humacao on the southeastern coast. It was just a little over an hour's drive from San Juan, but it felt worlds away from the capital. The southern half of the island was a lot more remote and less developed than the northern half. The villages were smaller, which I appreciated, having grown up in a small mountain town in British Columbia, and the jungle felt more imposing, as if the buildings and roads could barely keep it at bay.

We drove around, checking out different seaside communities. I was captivated by the beautiful Caribbean beaches as well as the majestic dormant volcanic mountains of the surrounding rainforest.

"I wonder if anyone has flown those," I said to Pam.

She just smiled. I suppose I was a little predictable after ten years together. She knew I'd have my paraglider up there soon enough.

But my main goal was to find places where I could kite surf. Kite surfing combines the thrills of both paragliding and surfing: you stand on your board and use the power of the wind in your canopy to propel you across the water. It's a sport I'd recently taught myself, and I intended to make the most of my time here mastering it. The majority of kiting is done on the north and southwest coasts of Puerto Rico; I hadn't found anything on the Internet about kiting near where we would be living. And that was fine by me, because I love a challenge, especially when it comes to doing something no one else has done.

As we explored more of the countryside, I became more optimistic about living in Puerto Rico. Besides the many adventure opportunities, I'd get to refocus on my art as well. If this scenery didn't inspire me, nothing would.

When we returned to our home in Rhode Island a few days later, I joked to Pam, "The door to this place won't get the chance to hit me on the ass on the way out."

As spring turned to summer turned to early fall, our move date was suddenly upon us. With packing help from my brother Barry, we escaped the predictability of Rhode Island for the unknown of Puerto Rico.

When the real estate agent provided by Pam's company brought us to the gated entrance of Palmas del Mar, the resort community in Humacao that would be our new home, I was stunned by the sheer size of the property. It was bigger than both Pam's and my hometowns combined. I didn't know then that it prided itself on being the largest planned community in the Caribbean, with banks and stores, two golf courses, a marina, a fancy private school, a casino, a country club, and twenty-four-hour security guards.

Although this was where most wealthy Puerto Ricans and expats lived in minimansions, we were able to secure a lease on a modest three-bedroom house that had enough room for visitors. There was also a small outbuilding shoehorned into the backyard that I could use as a studio. I felt more disappointed than privileged to be living the gated lifestyle, but I figured Pam's company knew best. Pam had heard from some of her coworkers on previous business trips to the island that house burglaries were common, and being in this community would keep us safer, or so we thought.

That first night in our new home, with most of our household belongings two months from joining us, it seemed like we had checked into a hotel rather than a new life.

"It feels like we're on vacation," I said.

"I know," said Pam. "Except I have to go to work on Monday."

"Well, it's not Monday yet. You wanna go to the beach?"

Palmas del Mar had its own gorgeous white sand beach, so we borrowed a golf cart—the vehicle of choice there—and made our way to the ocean in the late afternoon to enjoy the end of the beautiful day, listen to the waves lap gently against the sandy shore, and watch the spectacular sunset.

Yeah, this is home, I thought.

THREE

On Monday morning, while Pam readied herself for her first day in her new job, I loaded the car with my kite-surfing gear. Pam and I had agreed that I would take her to work in Juncos, a small city about thirty minutes away toward the center of the island, and pick her up in the evening. That way I'd have the vehicle to use during the day. I already had my sights set on a few beaches I had scoped out on Google Earth a few weeks earlier, and I was eager to check them out in person to see if they'd be good for kiting.

After dropping Pam off, I headed back east toward home, passing the exit for Palmas del Mar and continuing south into Yabucoa. I crossed a long bridge that traveled the width of the swampy valley before making a left toward Playa Lucia. From the satellite images I'd seen, the road would soon be obscured by jungle. Google didn't lie. A few moments after the turn, the road narrowed, and branches and leaves scraped along the sides of the truck. I was a little concerned about how I'd explain the new scratches back at the rental office when I turned the vehicle in. Luckily, I later learned that small scratches and dents were considered normal wear and tear here in Puerto Rico.

Eventually the jungle parted and I popped through the other side. The view before me was incredible: white sand, tall palm trees running the full length of the beach, and the aqua-colored sea beyond.

I couldn't wait to get my gear out of the truck, take out my little plastic wind meter to measure the wind speed and direction, and launch into the surf. I parked, strapped the gear to my back, and began my walk to the shore. My heart was racing with excitement.

I scanned my new surroundings, looking for obstacles or sea detritus that could pose a hazard. I needed to be extra careful since this was a new sport for me and I was doing it at an unfamiliar beach and, worse, without anyone else nearby in case I needed help—a bit of a no-no in extreme sports. Launching near a half-buried tree limb or one rusty old rowboat hidden by weeds could mean a bad stumble or worse, so I needed to get the lay of the land as best I could before hitting the waves. As I looked around, taking in the extraordinary beauty of the place, I started to notice a lot of garbage along the perimeter. I wondered how someone could just toss a McDonald's wrapper on the sand in such a beautiful place.

In the near distance, I spotted some sort of animal lying in the sand. I could kind of make out four legs and a skinny, furless tail, but that was all. I dropped my gear where I stood and headed toward it. As I got closer, my heart dropped and a wave of nausea surged through me. It was a dog, or what was left of one. His rib cage was visible through the sparse tufts of dark fur; he was so sunburned on the areas where fur had fallen out that the skin was split and bloody. His ears and snout were knobby and covered in calluses.

I looked around for something I could use as a shovel to bury him. I've always believed that every creature deserves dignity in death.

And then the dog raised his head and wagged his tail.

Aw, hell. How was this even possible?

"Hello, sweetie," I said, trying to keep my voice at a soothing level so as not to alarm the poor guy. He had clearly been through enough already. "What happened to you, sweetie?"

He stumbled to his feet as I approached, understandably wary of me. He was clearly weak and dehydrated.

"I'll help you, boy, don't worry."

My voice seemed to calm him, so I kept talking gently. In a few moments, he seemed less nervous. He wobbled back and forth on his feet and wagged his tail, drawing invisible figure eights in the air. I knelt beside him in the sand and cried. I couldn't imagine how anyone could have abandoned this poor, helpless dog on the beach. And yet he was friendly to a complete stranger.

Trying to guess his breed was nearly impossible, but I thought he might be part Siberian husky from his readily visible bone structure and, more distinctively, his eyes—one blue, one hazel. For a husky not to be readily identifiable, I thought, was horrifying.

I knew he would die soon, in a few days if not a few hours. It seemed to take all his energy just to stand for those few moments, so I gently guided him to a lying down position to rest. He folded up like a flimsy deck chair and sighed.

I stayed with him for a while, then decided to head for the store to get some dog food. "I'll be right back, okay, buddy?" I said, petting his disfigured head. I threw my gear back into the SUV and raced away from the beach, this time with no thought of what the jungle was doing to the SUV's paint job.

Problem was, I had no idea where to go. I hadn't been to this part of the island before. It was still pretty early in the morning, so I just hoped to find something open. Finally, I did.

Communicating with the store clerk was a bit of a challenge since I spoke no Spanish and few people, especially in rural areas, spoke English. But eventually I made my needs known and was pointed toward the baby aisle, where I grabbed a couple of bottles of Pedialyte, remembering that our vet had recommended it to us a few years earlier when our German shepherd was sick and dehydrated. A dog as emaciated as that husky had to be dehydrated too, I figured.

In the pet food area, I picked up several cans of wet dog food and a five-pound bag of dry food, figuring I should have it just in case, as well as some disposable dishes for the food and water.

Back at the beach, my new friend was still lying in the sand. He began wagging his tail when he saw me. As I approached, I noticed a few other dogs peeking out from the edge of the jungle. They stayed back, but seemed curious. As I bent down to get the food and water ready for the husky, I felt a nose brush my arm. It was attached to another small dog that wanted my attention. As I looked around, I counted about a dozen dogs standing around, tails wagging, waiting for breakfast. It seemed that while I was away, the husky had told a few of his friends that treats were on the way.

"I'm not going to have enough for all of you," I said, looking over the motley crew, all in varying stages of emaciation. I fed them everything I had. Then I headed back to the grocery store and cleaned out their dog food aisle. In the weeks to come, I would learn that wet food was easier on the dogs than dry. It doesn't bombard their nearly shut-down digestive systems and takes less energy to digest. I also learned to resist the urge to overfeed them, which would just make the dogs sick to their stomachs.

I arrived back to a hero's welcome. As I dished out more food and water, I couldn't help but notice how patient and polite the dogs were. They simply watched and waited for me to give the okay to start eating. It confirmed my suspicion that these dogs weren't mean or wild, as people tend to assume when they see strays on the street.

Many of the dogs had deep gashes or other open wounds. They didn't look like cuts from ducking under fences; they looked more like someone had cut them deliberately with a huge knife. The wounds were infected and packed with sand. A few had badly broken bones that had healed improperly. One little black female's front left paw pointed toward the sky; she used the second joint of her leg as a foot, her body twisting awkwardly when she walked. Another small female looked as if she'd been doused in gasoline and set on fire; her skin was charred and split everywhere. How could any of them stand to be around a human being?

I knew it was best to place the food down and step back to let the dogs eat and drink in peace, especially considering that I was dealing with street dogs that had likely been abused or dominated. Yet, as they ate, I began gently petting their backs and necks, slowly moving my hand toward the bowls of food to see if they had any food aggression. Considering that they were starving to death, I wouldn't have been surprised if they did. Instead, as I touched each one, it would pause from crunching away on the food to look up at me and wag its tail. There was no pausing, growling, or lifting of the lip in warning. It seemed they were just grateful I was there.

When they finished the last of the food and water, some of the dogs hobbled away from the dishes to relieve themselves. As they did, the diarrhea looked like someone had turned on a faucet full force and let it run. Dogs are generally sensitive to changes to their diet, so this wasn't surprising—even a well-tended family pet will often get diarrhea if its food is changed abruptly. That's why veterinarians advise that any change in a dog's food be made gradually, mixing the new food in with the old until the dog becomes acclimated. Obviously, I didn't have that luxury with these dogs. And unlike pets that have been well cared for, these dogs' feces were full of worms.

I found a spot of shade and sat down, my back against a palm tree. I had sixteen new friends now surrounding me. Some of them fell asleep with their heads in my lap; others dug cool holes in the sand nearby for a nap. Watching them rest, their legs twitching as they chased lizards in their dreams, I felt more anger than I knew how to manage. But I also felt more peace than I'd felt in ages. Already I felt like these were my dogs. I decided to start naming them, a task I took very seriously. I looked over at the tattered husky first, and asked him silently what I should call him—*Blue Eye,* he said. One down and fifteen to go.

Once I finished naming a few of them, I was struck by a much bigger question: What was I going to do with all these dogs? They needed more than food and water. They needed lifesaving medical treatment. If I left them here without helping, I knew for sure they would die.

I actually considered abandoning Playa Lucia to find another beach where I could kite surf. Perhaps I could just forget about the dogs and pretend like this morning's events had never happened. But as I sat with my new friends that afternoon, my mind carried me back to my childhood experience of the true love and loyalty of a dog. I remember saying to someone once, "We could learn a lot from dogs and their loyalty to their humans. Their ability to forgive is amazing."

Beyond that, there was a hole in my life since losing Achates earlier that year. I found myself wanting to make him proud and care for his brothers and sisters here on the beach. I couldn't replace him, but perhaps by doing what I could to save these lives, I could fill the void I felt without him at my side. I had no choice but to help the dogs. I knew deep in my heart that if I walked away, it would be a decision I'd regret the rest of my life.

I stayed there the better part of the day, gazing at an old abandoned boathouse in the distance, trying to figure out how I was going to follow through on this silent commitment I was making to the dogs, to Achates, to myself. First of all, I was going to need a lot of supplies.

As the sun moved across the sky, I knew I was going to have to pull myself away for the night. I hated the thought of leaving the pack that was now my responsibility. To make it worse, a couple of the pups tried to get into the truck when I opened the door. It was painfully obvious they didn't want to be left alone again, and, in a way, I could relate. As I started the engine, I looked to the side and saw every dog watching me go, their eyes begging me not to leave them. It actually hurt to see them looking so scared and abandoned. A few of them ran alongside the truck as I drove down the road, but stopped after a few yards, too weak to go any farther. I cried the whole drive back to the house.

I didn't know how I was going to manage it, but one thing was clear: the dogs needed me.

And I needed them. I just didn't know it yet.

FOUR

O n the way home, one other thing became crystal clear: I stank.

I'd had the dogs lying across my lap most of the day. They were all pretty smelly, especially the ones with mange or infected wounds. I hadn't really focused on anything but their nutrition until now. I was pretty sure the skin condition was Demodex, or demodectic mange, which is not contagious (unlike sarcoptic mange, which can be).

Demodex mites are normal parasites on many hosts. Generally they cause no problem because the host's immune system limits their growth. However, if the host is sick or has a compromised immune system, the mites can multiply quickly. When there are too many mites, their feeding destroys enough skin cells and hair follicles to make the fur fall out and the skin itchy, red, and often covered in festering boils. In addition, as the number of dead mites increases, both the skin damage and the decaying mites can cause bacterial infection in the skin. When a dog has a weakened immune system or is under extreme stress, it is more prone to this condition and slower to recover than a healthy dog.

When I got back to the house, I threw my filthy clothes into the washing machine and got showered as fast as I could. I called Pam at work to tell her what had happened.

"I'm going to need to get food and supplies for them. Are you okay with that? It might get a little expensive."

She didn't bat an eye. "Of course you can't leave them there. Do what you have to do. I'll find a ride home tonight. Good job, hon. I love you."

"I love you too. See you in a bit."

I rushed to Sam's Club, grabbed the biggest cart they had, and headed for the pet food aisle, where I loaded as many 55-pound bags as would fit. I then cruised the cleaning supplies aisle for disinfectant hand wipes, rubber gloves, and first aid supplies. I was no vet, and I'd had no formal training in animal rescue. I was guided largely by intuition and past experience with my own dogs, as well as the EMT certification I'd received years ago as part of my mountaineering and paragliding instructor training.

The checkout lanes were at least ten customers deep, and I worried I wouldn't make it to the pharmacy next door before closing time at six o'clock. But just as I was about to stash the cart and run out to grab medical supplies first, a young cashier looked at the mountain of dog food in my cart, smiled, and motioned for me to follow her. She opened a new register, and while she scanned my items, asked where I was from.

"I haven't seen you in the store before," she said. She explained that she was originally from New Jersey, but her family had moved to Puerto Rico when she was in her teens.

"Why so much dog food?"

I told her what had happened at the beach and a little about the dogs.

She shook her head. "It's a problem all over the island," she said. "People don't respect animals here." As I pushed my cart toward the exit, she added, "Welcome to Puerto Rico. Good luck!"

At the pharmacy next door, I bought all the dewormer, dog shampoo, and appropriate medical supplies they had.

It was already dark when I was putting everything into the truck, and rain had started to fall. Hard. As I drove away, the thunder and lightning was so intense it rattled the truck. The wipers couldn't keep up with the torrents of rain coming down. But I was safe and dry inside the vehicle, and all I could think about was the dogs alone at the beach with no protection from the elements. I remembered how scared Achates would get during a storm.

The rain stopped as quickly as it had begun. I arrived home just as Pam was being dropped off by a coworker. I was feeling very emotional, so I kept the small talk to a minimum while I unloaded the truck. I've learned over the years that it's best to keep to myself when I'm overwrought so I don't overreact and say something I'll regret.

I finally recounted the day's events to Pam as we were getting supper ready. I told her I couldn't believe how sweet the dogs were, considering how badly beaten they appeared to be. Talking to Pam about it was like seeing it all through a different set of eyes and helped me process everything I'd seen. I flipped through mental images of the different dogs. The sadness felt like a hole in my chest.

"Be careful out there," she said. "You don't know the island."

"I'll be extra vigilant. Don't worry."

As if that made any difference. Of course she'd worry.

I was awakened during the night by another heavy storm. The pounding rain and cacophonous thunder were like nothing I'd ever experienced. I thought of the dogs at the beach and how terrified they must be. I didn't sleep much after that. I knew from my experience in wilderness survival that when you don't feel well, even when the air temperature is warm, you still feel cold and miserable. Most of those dogs had little to no hair and were suffering from severe malnutrition, so they must be in excruciating misery. I hoped they had at least found shelter in the abandoned boathouse on the beach.

When the alarm went off in the morning, I was exhausted, but I sprang to my feet in anticipation of what I needed to do that day. As Pam got ready for work, I loaded the truck with the food, water, and medical supplies I'd picked up the night before. I planned to head straight back to the beach after I dropped her off at work.

As I left Pam at the gated entrance to her workplace, she said, "Watch your back, okay?"

Aside from all the warnings Pam's coworkers had already given us about being careful outside Palmas del Mar, Pam had been talking with one of the local women at her office about what I'd found at the beach. The woman had immediately expressed concern for my safety and suggested that Pam persuade me to steer clear of that area. I didn't really understand why, but in time it would become all too clear.

"I'll check in every few hours, I promise," I told Pam, even though I'd noticed the day before that I didn't get much of a cell phone signal at the beach.

I flew down the highway toward the coast, anxious to see how the dogs had fared during the night. I had butterflies in my stomach as I drove the final long stretch of jungle road to the beach. I hoped I wouldn't be burying Blue Eye or any of the others today.

CHAPTER FIVE

A s I parked on the edge of the sand, I spotted a few dogs stretching and yawning. They looked tired but happy to see me as I got out of the truck. As I would learn over the coming weeks, the dogs had learned to hide in the sand or along the perimeter of the jungle. You only saw them if they wanted you to. I looked around for the dogs I'd been with the day before.

Blue Eye lay curled up in a ball in the sand. I wondered if my fears of finding him dead had come to pass. "Hey, Blue Eye!" I called out to him. I didn't expect him to know his name—I just wanted to get his attention. He raised his head and staggered to his feet. I rushed over so he didn't have so far to travel.

He wagged his bony, hairless tail and pranced around with excitement as best he could. He couldn't bend his legs properly. He had no muscle mass to control his limbs, so he looked like a stick-figure drawing wobbling around. It was painful to watch him expend so much energy just to greet me.

I slowly made my way back to the truck to get the supplies out of the back.

I organized the bowls so that each dog had his own dish of dry food mixed with canned soft food. All the dogs sat patiently waiting for their breakfast.

There were a few new faces. A large male I had seen the day before was standing off to the side, quietly observing. He was covered in battle scars across his face and body; some of them looked like they had been inflicted by humans. This old guy hadn't let me pet him yet, but I figured he'd come around when he felt more comfortable. I had a feeling he was a good dog. Despite his wounds, he was in far better condition than many of the others. His stoic nature was likely what had kept him alive. The other dogs watched him as he watched me, following his lead. I suspected he was most likely the leader of this pack of strays.

I set the feeding bowls down and watched how the dogs behaved. Some were so excited by the prospect of food that they spun in circles. Others sat patiently, fanning the sand and gravel with their tails, waiting for my okay. The puppies couldn't contain themselves and dove right in, wolfing down the food and water, stepping and sitting in the bowls, spilling food all over the place. There was no sign of a mother.

Blue Eye and some of the weaker dogs ate more respectfully and slowly. They felt no need to rush. As I had the day before, I put my hand on their heads and then slowly moved it toward their bowls; they'd lift their heads for a moment and try to lick my hand and face, then return to munching. They showed no signs of aggression toward me whatsoever.

The temptation of the food, water, and attention was becoming too much for the big leader, but still he kept his distance. I walked away from the bowls and pretended to do something in the back of the vehicle. I watched through the side window of the truck as he took the opportunity to approach the feeding area. As he walked forward, the others respectfully parted and made way for him. He went from bowl to bowl, tasting from each. As he ate, the more experienced dogs backed off and waited for him to finish. Some of the young males attempted to challenge him, going for the food before he gave the signal that it was okay. The large dog bared his teeth and growled, but it ended immediately. Order was reestablished. The only wounds were to the younger dogs' pride. They would have to eat last.

The feeding ritual went on day after day through the next week. I knew

I had to gain the trust of the alpha dog in order to be fully accepted by the pack. Slowly but surely, he began to warm up. He still wouldn't let me near enough to pet him, but I knew that if I was patient and waited, I would have a friend for life. I loved the challenge of seeing how far I could push them without scaring them off. I've always felt that in order to get past one's fears and heal, one needs to confront the very thing that caused the fears to begin with. I remembered having similar feelings about the challenge of working with orphaned children in Southeast Asia. I knew I had my work cut out for me, but I loved it.

SIX

For five nights straight, Pam listened to my stories about the dogs.

"Will you come with me this weekend?" I asked Friday evening when I picked her up from work.

"Absolutely. I'd like to put faces to all these dogs you keep talking about."

"It's not pretty, you know that, right?"

As we drove down the isolated road toward the beach the following morning, I prepared her as best I could for what she was going to see.

"But watch what they do when we get there," I said afterward, to give her something positive to look forward to. I wanted her to understand why I'd gotten so attached.

As soon as they heard my truck, the dogs, some of which had established their own little routine of waiting for me at the entrance to the beach each morning, came running (and tottering, limping, and dragging—whatever they could manage). They followed alongside until I came to a stop. I gave a little whistle (which I modeled after the coquis' cry) to summon the dogs that hadn't heard the truck. As Pam and I got out, they were all around us, excited to see me and curious about this new person I'd brought for them to sniff.

For Pam, it was love at first sight. It appeared the feeling was mutual.

Years earlier, when we lived in California, Pam had volunteered at a local shelter. She wasn't afraid of dogs of any size. But it didn't take long for reality to sink in. Within moments of our arrival, tears were rolling down her face. Even after everything I'd told her, she hadn't imagined what bad shape the dogs were in.

"I just want to hold them," she said crying. It was killing her that she couldn't, but the wounds on some of them made it too painful for them to be touched. It was also likely that many of them had never known the loving hand of a kind human. Yet they seemed to sense her pain and tried to comfort her, wagging their tails and nuzzling her arms and legs with their noses. The dogs' selflessness in looking after a human—a stranger—confirmed why I needed to do everything I could to ease their suffering.

We spent the morning sitting with them in the sand as they fell asleep. Their physical condition hadn't improved, but their spirits seemed brighter than when I'd found them at the beginning of the week. Even the sickest ones in the group had a new sparkle in their eyes.

"It's so obvious it's not about the food, Steve," Pam said. "They just want our attention."

She was right. Even with everything these dogs had clearly been through, human kindness was still their greatest reward.

And then the real miracle happened. The big leader came up behind Pam and nudged her arm, asking for a pet. After watching me interact with his pack all week, he was finally ready to get some affection. After Pam had stroked him a bit, he let me caress his face.

By early afternoon, this isolated beach started to come to life with other humans. When I came during the week, the beach was a ghost town. The only people I'd seen were the occasional fisherman or someone in an official-looking car from the local municipality driving by slowly and staring at me with the dogs. But now a dozen families were there setting up for a picnic. As the crowd and noise escalated, the dogs became upset and started to pace.

Before I knew what was happening, a couple of guys on motorcycles were racing around, narrowly missing the dogs and us. Pam and I stood up to gather our things and pack the truck. Just off to the side, we heard a hollow thud followed by yelping and the sound of someone laughing. As I turned to look, I saw a dog running away from a guy throwing rocks. Without thinking, I ran between the guy and the dog.

"What the hell are you doing?" I screamed, throwing my hands up in the air.

He laughed for a moment until he realized I wasn't joking.

"Get back here!" I heard Pam yell. But I wasn't going to back down. The rock thrower and I stared each other down for a minute until he started to look uncomfortable and walked away.

As I turned to walk back to the truck, I was a little surprised to see the pack leader and some of the stronger, healthier dogs at my side. I had been so focused on the guy throwing rocks that I hadn't seen them. They hadn't made a sound.

I knelt down to give them a pat. "Thank you for standing by me," I told them. It was clear that they were as intent on protecting me as I was them. As I looked into the big leader's eyes, I remembered a large stuffed animal my grandparents had given me when I was a young boy. Leo the Lion had been my protector when I was afraid to be alone after my dad died. The big leader had found his name: Leo, King of the Beach.

Pam and I left with tears streaming down our cheeks. As we pulled away, I noticed in the rearview mirror that the dogs weren't following the truck like they had before. Instead, they disappeared into the dense jungle, as if they knew it wasn't safe for them on the beach once I left.

When we returned the next morning, there were a few new dogs on the beach, watching us from a distance. They never worked up the courage to approach us, but I figured they would in time. What was more unusual was that some of the familiar dogs didn't show up when I brought out breakfast.

"Stay here, I'm going to have a look around," I told Pam. As the pack ate, she kept them company while I headed down the beach looking for the strag-glers. The search, however, was a bust. I just assumed they had found food elsewhere that day. I'd have to look again tomorrow.

Just like on Saturday, the beach got busy by early afternoon—cars and motorcycles zipping around, loud music pounding, people drinking and screaming. Some beachgoers chased the dogs away to make room for their hammocks. As we started to pack the supplies into the truck, the dogs sensed it was time to take shelter and retreated to the jungle as we headed out.

I couldn't put my finger on it, but I had a bad feeling in the pit of my stom-ach as we drove home that afternoon.

SEVEN

Monday morning, there was no sign of the weekend revelers. I was alone with the pack again. However, the missing dogs from Sunday didn't show up for the morning feeding again. So afterward, I went in search of them by foot.

I started walking down the single-track road to the left of the beach entrance, trailed by a few of the dogs. It was a narrow, overgrown road that led deeper into the jungle. I'd often seen dogs emerging from there when I arrived each morning. It was peppered with rain-filled potholes and crowded with dense jungle growth. As I made my way along, pushing branches and vines to the side, the dogs followed. I soon picked up the sweet-putrid smell of death wafting in on the sea breeze from my right.

As I moved closer to the stench, I was stopped by a tall, vine-covered chain-link fence. On the other side, I saw the weed-riddled parking lot of the abandoned boathouse that had been left to the elements and the dogs. I'd seen the boathouse's enormous metal corrugated walls and roof from the main beach before, but I'd never ventured close enough to go in. The smell of decay was so strong I could taste it in the back of my throat. I slid my sweat-soaked shirt up over my nose to quiet my gag reflex. It helped, but only a little. Looking through the diamond mesh of the fence, I saw three of my dogs lying motionless on the ground. They looked as though they'd been beaten with a baseball bat. I could see rocks embedded in their broken bodies, and other large rocks scattered nearby.

They must have been trying to escape under the fence to get away from whoever had been chasing them. One of the young females had managed to get only halfway under the fence before she was killed. Her body blocked the escape route for the two dogs that lay dead behind her.

I laced my fingers through the rusting fence and held on, waves of nausea swelling up from my belly. It wasn't just the smell that was making me feel ill; it was the sight of my friends' broken bodies. I could only imagine the fear they must have felt as they were chased and tortured so brutally. I was overwhelmed with a fierce mixture of sadness and anger that made me dry heave.

The dogs behind me whined and paced anxiously. I slid down the fence onto my knees. The dogs nudged my elbows, trying to lift my arms to pet them.

I gathered myself and stood up. I needed to bury my dogs. They deserved in death the dignity they had been denied in life. But they were decomposing fast in the tropical heat, and there was no way I could carry them someplace appropriate to bury them. I walked back along the path again until it rejoined the main road to the beach. I turned into the entrance of the parking lot and made for the boathouse, figuring there might be something there I could use to carry sand from the beach. I found a five-gallon pail and returned to the beach to fetch sand. It would take a number of trips to bring enough back to where the dogs lay motionless. Leo and the others followed me as I trudged back and forth. It took more than an hour to bury my friends.

Burials would become part of my daily routine at the beach. Every morning I'd find new dogs, and every morning I'd go in search of missing members of the pack. Every time I found another dead dog, its corpse was a heap of severely broken bones or had been cut into pieces and stuffed into plastic buckets or garbage bags. It was usually the dogs that had been less cautious of humans. I buried at least one dog every day.

The dogs would watch quietly as I buried their friends. Despite all the things humans had done to them, the pack continued to trust me.

We had been living in Puerto Rico for about three weeks when my friend Brandon, a nineteen-year-old whom I'd met at an indoor climbing gym in Rhode Island the previous winter, came to visit.

The prospect of having some fun with a fellow athlete and adventure seeker, was just what I needed. Pam was having a tough time adjusting to her new life. She was feeling a bit homesick, under a lot of pressure at work, worried about my frequent visits to the beach and my growing involvement with the dogs. Frankly, I also needed a break from the heart-rending things I'd seen since moving to the island.

The morning after Brandon arrived, we made plans to go snorkeling at Seven Seas Beach, which was about forty-five minutes from the house. But first I asked him if he'd like to meet my dogs.

"Whoa, man, there are a lot more here than I expected," he said as we pulled into the parking lot near the boathouse. The pack had nearly doubled since I'd first described it to him.

The dogs, with their uncanny sixth sense, immediately pegged Brandon for a good guy and bonded with him right away. We spent the morning hanging out with the pack, and Brandon helped me name a few dogs that I hadn't been able to come up with appropriate monikers for yet. Then we hit the road.

I'd never been to the place we were going, and the incomplete, cartoonish road map Pam and I had gotten from the car rental depot in San Juan was no help whatsoever. Most of the roads we needed to travel weren't even on it, and Brandon wasn't much help since he'd never been outside the continental United States before. So we tooled around Fajardo, the community near where the Seven Seas Beach was supposed to be located. After several wrong turns through some questionable neighborhoods, we found our spot, a beautiful crescent-shaped bay begging us to get in and explore.

We parked on a side street, grabbed our snorkeling gear, and made for the far end of the beach on foot, knowing there'd be better snorkeling by the reef. Since it was a weekday, there were just a few folks walking the shoreline. We would have the water to ourselves.

In the distance, waves were breaking over the barrier reef. We jumped in and swam out to where the action was. We spent a good hour snorkeling through the intricate paths of coral mapped out on the sea floor, using the gentle surges and currents to propel ourselves through the valleys of undersea architecture. Every few minutes, we surfaced to compare notes.

"Dude! Did you see the sea turtles back there?"

"Amazing, man! Or the big manta ray?"

"I know, so awesome!"

"Let's keep swimming, man!"

We seemed to be seeing and thinking the same things. It was fantastic.

Then we noticed some men spearfishing on the reef closer to shore. We weren't anywhere near them, so we didn't give them another thought, focusing instead on the incredible theater below.

The next time we surfaced, the men were standing on the reef right over us, homemade tridents and spearguns in their hands.

"Hey, how's it going, man?" we said, and gave them a friendly wave. The men said nothing; they just stared at us coldly. They didn't seem to be fishing anymore. I had that foreboding feeling I'd had many times in the past, right before things went south. Something wasn't right.

During my short time on the island, it had already become apparent that Puerto Rico was struggling between two worlds. Since it's an unincorporated territory of the United States, the residents are American citizens, but they don't have all the same rights that Americans living in the States do. They can't vote for the president and aren't even represented in Congress, but they *can* be drafted into the military. Approximately half the islanders want to be independent from the United States, and the other half want to be the fifty-first state. The former group tends to be pretty hostile to non-Puerto Ricans living on the island. Anti-American demonstrations weren't uncommon during our time there. The international school in Palmas del Mar, where we lived, and another in San Juan were shut down due to bomb threats more than once.

Living in this strange limbo has taken its toll on the Puerto Rican people. The crime rate was already high, but got worse when the military shut down its bases on the island. During the twentieth century, there were as many as twenty-five different installations, but the Air Force and Navy left, leaving just the U.S. Coast Guard and Puerto Rico National Guard facilities. Those bases had been a boon to the local economy, as were big companies like the one my wife was working for, but they were starting to shut down their local facilities too. For all the protests about the weapons training facility that had been located on the Puerto Rican island of Vieques, when the military pulled up stakes there and elsewhere in the early years of the millennium, a lot of residents felt it in their pocketbooks. The median income in Puerto Rico is about half what it is in Mississippi, the poorest of the fifty states.

But the vast majority of people don't react by threatening visitors. The spearfishermen might have been pissed off that we invaded their locals-only space, but I had a feeling there was more to it than that.

"C'mon, man, let's get outta here!" I said to Brandon.

"Naw, let's keep swimming, dude!" He clearly wasn't getting the bad vibe I was from our new neighbors.

"Brandon," I said a little more urgently, "we need to get back to our stuff." We'd left some gear and our towels on the beach.

He quit arguing, and we started making our way back to shore through the maze of coral. But after just a few minutes, we looked up and saw the men standing on the reef right next to us again.

"Aw, shit," I said under my breath. Brandon had continued swimming and was a short distance away from me now, still exploring the reef. "Brandon! We need to go . . . now!"

I felt something sharp poke my lower back. I pretended not to notice. I put my snorkel in my mouth, dropped my face into the water, and started to swim.

A harder jab this time, on the back of my surf shorts. I looked up to see one of the guys with a trident towering over me.

"How's it going, bro?" I said. "You catch any fish yet?" I smiled and waved. "Have a good day, man!"

Brandon was starting to catch on, and we swam away as fast as we could, slipping through narrow coral pathways we normally would have avoided. But these fishermen, or whatever the hell they were, obviously knew the reef much better than we did. At every turn, these assholes were right behind us or alongside us.

We put our heads down and made a last hard push to get to shore as quickly as possible. As we sprinted out of the water and looked around, the men were gone.

"Where the hell are they?" I said, catching my breath from the swim.

And that's when we noticed that our stuff was gone as well. They'd taken everything, even our shoes and towels. Fortunately, I had stashed my truck keys under a rock a few yards from where we'd left our things on the beach. Otherwise, we'd have been screwed.

"Aw, man. They took all our shit," Brandon said.

"Forget it, man. Let's just get the hell out of here."

We hightailed it down the beach toward the truck, wondering if the guys were going to jump us along the way. The beach was hot as hell and covered in pebbles and small shells, tearing and cutting into the soles of our feet. At the entrance there was a small park and a lookout area with benches. Sure enough, the ass-hats were sitting there, waiting for us.

"Amigos! You looking for something?" They said something else in Spanish, but hell if I knew or even cared what it was. One of the men held up my gear bag, a big shit-eating grin on his face.

"What are you going to do, man?" Brandon asked me, as if I were actually going to take on a couple of guys carrying spearguns.

"Not a goddamn thing," I said.

I'd learned before we even moved to Puerto Rico that most robberies and thefts are committed against tourists because they're suspected of carrying more cash than the locals. Local thieves also know that foreign visitors generally don't pursue charges once they find out what's involved. In order to press charges or file a theft report, the victim must be willing to sign a contract with the police stating that if the criminal is apprehended, the victim will return to the island for the trial at his or her own expense. If for some reason the victim will not or cannot return to testify, the Puerto Rican government will issue an arrest warrant for the victim for failing to appear. And who's going to take the time and incur the expense of coming back for a lost camera or, worse, risk going to jail themselves?

In other words, I knew these guys were going to get away with it—and I knew they knew it too.

"We need to get to the truck fast, okay?" I said. "On three, you run your goddamn ass off. You drop something, you leave it behind. Am I clear?"

One of the other men waved more of our things at us, laughing.

Brandon and I looked at each other. "Three! Go! Go! Go!" I may have been a lot older, but I could still outrun a teenager when I needed to. The men stood up and raced after us.

I clicked the door locks open with the remote, and we jumped in and locked the doors behind us. Safely inside, the engine running, we realized the men had given up the chase about halfway to the truck. We should have been relieved, but we quickly realized we'd been outmaneuvered again. The road we were parked on dead-ended fifty yards up the road at the entrance to a lighthouse located at the end of the peninsula. There was only one way out. And not only were the men standing across the two-lane road in front of us blocking it, but they had evidently picked up a few friends.

"Let's see how they do against twenty-five hundred pounds of metal and plastic." I put the truck in gear and floored it, heading straight for the human roadblock. "You up for a little bowling?"

Brandon was too scared to laugh and smiled nervously.

The human chain parted at the last second, and we flew through the gap. Gobs of spit splattered the windshield, and we heard the sounds of their hands slapping the sides of the truck as we passed. My heart was beating in my neck. Brandon's had practically stopped beating. Escaping hostile spearfishermen and bursting through human roadblocks weren't exactly the extreme sports he'd had in mind when he came to visit.

After we'd returned home and told Pam what had happened, she said, "What makes you think you'll be able to get away safely the next time something like this happens? This could have ended so badly, Steve. This just freaks me out."

The stress of finding and burying dead dogs each day, along with tending to the sick, injured, and starving that were somehow still alive, was beginning to take a toll on me—and Pam was starting to question my judgment. She knew me too well.

Early one morning after Brandon left, I stood leaning on my shovel, looking out across the grassy field between the beach and the boat-house. It was the area I'd designated as the graveyard. An elderly local fisherman named Carlos and his wife, Dominga, approached me.

"Are you okay, *mi hijo?*" Carlos asked in his gruff voice.

Up until that moment I had been lost in thought and not really aware that anyone else was there. Apparently they'd seen me carrying one of the dogs across the parking lot to bury her.

"I'm okay, thanks," I said, without really looking up.

"We've seen how you are with the *satos,* feeding them and taking care of them. You're a good man." Carlos patted my shoulder. "I know it's hard when they die like that."

By now I'd learned that *sato* was the local term for a street dog, which some Puerto Ricans tended to use with a dismissive sneer. It essentially trans-lates to "street mutt," and I never used it myself. I had come to think of the dogs at the beach simply as *my dogs*. At that point, I thought that no one else was willing to take responsibility for them, so they were mine.

"Be careful here, son," his wife said. "There are people who come to this beach who could kill you if you get in their way, and they won't bat an eye at doing it."

I wondered who could possibly want to kill me simply for taking care of innocent strays. But as we talked further, I thought of the sketchy-looking people I'd seen hanging out in the shadows of the boathouse. The interactions were pretty quick—cars drove up, people passed objects I couldn't make out through the windows, and they sped away minutes later. I'd even seen police cars roll up and meet with the shady characters in the darkness of the dilapidated structure. I assumed the figures were drug dealers because I couldn't fathom any other reason people would come to this derelict dead-end part of the world. But I minded my own business like I hadn't seen anything. If they passed close by, I'd give a friendly wave. But my instincts, which had sharpened again since moving to Puerto Rico, were telling me to be more careful.

"Listen, *mi hijo*," Carlos said. "You're not in the States anymore. You had better watch your back. You could go missing here and no one would ever find you. It happens all the time." He sounded like he was pissed off at me, but I knew he was actually being emphatic out of concern.

I thanked them both and assured them I would heed their warning and try to be careful.

But first I had to find the puppies of the mother that the old couple had just seen me bury. I went back to where I had found her lying at the edge of the parking lot near the tall grass. I was pretty sure she'd made her den there. I'd found her with a half-eaten hot dog in her mouth; she'd clearly been poisoned. By then I'd heard that people on the island fed unwanted animals something called "two step," which caused a fast but violent death moments after ingesting it. I needed to see if the pups had made it or if they too were gone.

I rummaged through the grass, listening for sounds of life. And then I heard it: the telltale squeaks and grunts of baby dogs. The grass was so thick I couldn't see them, so I had to be careful where I stepped. I dropped to my hands and knees, feeling around until I finally found three little ones. I estimated them to be a couple of weeks old at most. Their eyes weren't even open yet. I gently gathered them up and put them inside my shirt to keep warm and hear my heartbeat. They yelped, squeaked, and grunted for their mother. They would die if I didn't do something.

A few days earlier, I'd discovered another nursing mother, who had made a den in the safety of the jungle just off the main road. A couple of her pups had died. She had whimpered and whined when, not wanting her remaining puppies to get sick, I took the dead ones out from under her. I hoped I could introduce these new pups to her and she would take them as her own. I had seen this done when I was kid, and I had a feeling it would work now if I handled the introductions properly.

As I approached, the mother dog immediately noticed the puppy noises coming from inside my shirt. She nudged at the squirming bundle, and sniffed their little bodies stem to stern. After a few minutes, she settled down with her own puppies and gave me a look that seemed to say, "I'll take them. Those are my puppies now." I placed the orphans by her side, and in no time they were nursing happily. The mom licked, cleaned, and prodded at them as they suckled. I stayed with her and the puppies for the rest of the day, my heart swelling with elation as I watched the puppies heal the mother and the mother save these orphans.

But a dark thought clouded my happiness: Was I really doing these puppies any good, or was I just postponing the inevitable?

CHAPTER NINE

I had become a creature of habit, going through my daily routine without fail. I arrived at the entrance to the beach every morning after dropping Pam off at work. I combed the long road, looking for newly dumped dogs. I put out the dishes for food and water, working to gain the trust of the new arrivals. The new ones were usually scared, hungry, thirsty, and badly abused, so I was very careful about introducing the new dogs to the pack before they were ready.

I figured their abusers were most likely men, so I knew I had my work cut out for me to gain their trust. The existing pack already respected me as their alpha, and I needed to make sure there was harmony among the members at all times. It was important that the new ones found their proper place in this ragtag family without too much trouble. If they fought after I left each evening, the injuries would mean almost certain death due to infection, so I did everything I could to ensure that didn't happen. I'd often stay for hours into the evening after an already long day spent working with the dogs, correcting problems before they escalated, like when a new dog's skittishness stirred up the pack. But there was power in the pack; if there was cohesion among the dogs, they would protect one another when I wasn't there to help them. Like people, dogs don't do as well alone; they survive better as a pack.

Determined to do something to stop the human violence, I decided to pay a visit to the police station in Yabucoa to ask if they'd conduct more patrols of the beach area to deter whoever was killing the dogs. Their response: "Sorry, no English." Even when I returned armed with the correct Spanish phrases, I still received blank stares.

Puerto Rico has no animal control officers or dog registry, and no government agency is assigned direct responsibility for the strays. While animal cruelty laws do exist, they're simply not enforced. To many people, especially those who live off the land, an animal is just an animal. And it's not just dogs, it's all animals—horses, cats, roosters, manatees.

A family might even adopt or buy a puppy or kitten only to find the expense and time involved in owning a pet too much to handle. Then they'll abandon their pet to the wild or even kill it. There are only a handful of privately run shelters in Puerto Rico, and, as I was coming to learn, Playa Lucia was far from the only place where dogs were abandoned. This island paradise, home to four million people and host to another three million tourists each year, had something on the order of a quarter of a million stray and abandoned dogs roaming the streets and jungle, looking for food and shelter. It seemed there was nobody in this community, or any other for that matter, willing to do anything about it.

It was becoming a nearly overwhelming effort to drag myself out of the house in the morning because of what I'd likely find when I got to the beach. I often wished I had the fortitude, or maybe the callousness, to walk away from the mess and go paragliding or kite surfing. The death toll kept climbing. Every drive to the beach was filled with the dread of wondering which dog would be missing that day.

And then, one morning, it was Blue Eye who didn't show up. The first dog I befriended on that godforsaken beach and, until that day, still the first to greet me when I arrived each morning. There had been a bad rain the night before, and, as was often the case after a storm, the dogs were acting a bit off. I'd learned by now that they often took shelter in the boathouse when the weather was bad. I decided to have a look to see if Blue Eye, who was still in pretty rough shape, was hiding out there.

At the door, I slid my sunglasses on top of my head and let my eyes adjust to the dim light inside. The concrete floor was covered with broken glass and puddles where the roof leaked. Across the room, I spotted a lifeless pile of bones and fur. I recognized him instantly. I was taken back to that first day at the beach, when I found what looked like a pile of seaweed or coconut husks in the sand that ended up becoming my new friend. The room grew blurry through the veil of tears in my eyes. I went to him and knelt by his side, caressing his face. I stayed like that for a long time, saying good-bye to this lovely dog who had worked his magic, found his way into my heart, and given me a new purpose.

By the time I stood up, my feet had fallen asleep and my knees ached. The entire pack, about forty dogs now, stood around me. They followed as I walked to the truck to grab my shovel and returned to the boathouse, where I found a rubber pool liner hidden behind some old shipping containers. I wrapped Blue Eye in the liner, carried him to the burial ground, and started to dig.

When the hole was large enough, I put my friend inside. As I threw the first shovelful of sand over his body, my courage and determination drained. I felt sick to my stomach and numb, like part of me had died and was being buried with him. I wondered how many more deaths I could bear. I thought of all the other dogs from the beach, of Tanya and Achates, of my father and grandfather.

When it was done, I wrestled with the urge to run as I had as a boy. But I didn't. Not this time. Instead, I just sat quietly with the pack and said good-bye to my friend. They needed me to be strong, and I was beginning to realize how much I needed them too. I was exhausted from emotion. I collapsed in the sand, leaning against a palm tree, drifting off to sleep, the pack hovering and watching over me.

I was awakened when the dogs jumped up suddenly and bolted a few yards away. As I rolled to the side to stand up, I was stopped short by a hollow thump and an excruciating bolt of pain in my back and shoulder that left me breathless.

"What the hell?" I turned to see who had struck me with such force. I expected to see one of the thugs I'd encountered earlier standing over me with a baseball bat. I only saw the dogs, concerned looks on their faces. Oddly, they hadn't run for the jungle. That's when I saw a fresh green coconut the size of a football lying in the sand next to where I'd been sitting.

I learned a couple of valuable lessons that day. The first was never to sit under a coconut tree laden with fruit. The second was that dogs are way more aware of their surroundings than humans. I was lucky to have only a big bruise on my back and ribs rather than a fractured skull or spine.

After that day, I made it a point to visit the boathouse as part of my daily routine. One morning I found five dogs lying dead next to the massive rusting shipping containers, against the fence of the west exterior wall of the building, one of the containers leaning precariously on an old tractor tire. Two of the dogs had been dismembered with machetes. The others had apparently been stoned to death, their skulls and chests crushed. I started back toward the truck for the shovel that I had become far too familiar with, when I spied a police cruiser parked along the side road parallel to the sandy beach. The cops may have dismissed me when I went to the station house, but it would be a lot harder to ignore me now. I could show them firsthand what I was talking about.

I walked up to the vehicle, but it was hard to see inside past the palm trees reflected in the closed windows. I leaned in and shielded my eyes with my hands. The officer's eyes were closed. I tapped on the window to wake him.

The cop shot up in his seat like a rocket. So did a very young girl in a Catholic school uniform who was bent over his lap.

In seconds, the cop had thrown open the cruiser door and was screaming at me while he fastened his pants. Once his zipper was secure, his right hand came to rest on the service piece on his hip.

I took a step back, my hands in front of me in a supplicant's posture. I didn't understand a word he was screaming at me, but I wanted to defuse the situation as fast as I could. The girl in the passenger seat was crying, trying to straighten her skirt and blouse.

After a few minutes the cop had yelled himself out and got back in the car. That was when I noticed that the dogs had been at my side the whole time, quietly growling, hackles raised. Between the girl and my pack, no wonder the cop backed off. As he sped away, spewing gravel and sand in his wake, I was sure I hadn't seen the last of him.

CHAPTER TEN

I think someone else is feeding the dogs," I told Pam one night over dinner.

I had recently started finding little piles of dog food in different areas of the beach. If it had been a onetime thing, I might have disregarded it as a fluke, some beachgoer taking rare pity on the dogs. But it was becoming a regular occurrence. The more I expanded my explorations of the area, the more I kept discovering the small mounds, hidden from plain view.

One morning after doing my rounds with the pack, I followed the trail of kibble down the beach until I found the source. A short distance ahead, I spotted a young Puerto Rican woman holding a bag of dog food in her arms with several of my smaller dogs at her feet.

I extended my hand to shake and said, "Hey, how's it going. I'm Stephen."

She smiled and shook my hand warmly. "I know. Everybody knows who *you* are," she said.

Fortunately for me, Sandra, a local schoolteacher, spoke very good English, so I started to pepper her with questions. Her work with the dogs became even more impressive to me when she explained that she and her husband, Angel, struggled to afford their own food, let alone food for so many dogs.

"Do you know why so many dogs get dumped here?" I asked.

"It's not just here. In the jungle too and other beaches and by the road. All over the island really."

"Why?"

"One day the puppy is so cute, but then it grows up, it's not so cute anymore. And it is too much trouble. . . ." She shrugged rather than finish her thought out loud. "I don't ask too many questions. I don't want no trouble. I just want to help the dogs."

It was enough. I understood.

Finally I felt like I had an ally here.

Late one afternoon, not long after I'd met Sandra for the first time, I bumped into another dog guardian at the beach. Like Sandra, Sonia was a schoolteacher by day, but in the evenings and on weekends, she volunteered at a privately run dog shelter in Humacao called El Faro dog rescue, which was run by a Catholic nun called Sister Nancy. Sonia had a huge heart, and the dogs really seemed to love her. It made me happy to know that someone else was watching over them too. Having her around as well as Sandra gave me hope.

Three days before Christmas, I was doing my rounds when Peggy, a young mother dog, came running to me barking frantically. I could see fear and panic in her eyes. Until now, Peggy had kept her distance and made it clear that she didn't trust humans. I could tell from her engorged teats that she had nursing pups hidden somewhere on the beach, but I had never been able to find her den.

She whimpered and barked at me, then ran toward the main road. I dropped everything and followed her.

On the edge of the road, a man was clearing the undergrowth with a backhoe. For the last few days, I'd seen a work crew widening the road to the beach. The jungle had closed in, scratching and damaging vehicles that dared to venture down it.

Peggy darted past the workers and started digging frantically at the over-turned soil. It took a split second before I understood what was happening and yelled, "Stop!" I barreled past the backhoe and joined Peggy, desperately scrabbling at the dirt, trying to unearth her litter. When the workers realized what had happened, they too began digging with bare hands and shovels. The first pup uncovered had a crushed skull. The next three were gasping for air, but okay. One was yelping in pain from an obvious compound fracture of his leg. The last one had been buried too long. I turned to look at the men. They stood quietly, heads down, tears visible.

I needed help, so I fired off a call to Sandra, but it went to voice mail. A short while later, she arrived and helped me find a safe place for Peggy and her surviving puppies. After we moved her brood, Peggy looked exhausted and desperate, so we let her rest.

Unfortunately, it was Pam's birthday. I called her while she was at work to explain what had happened with Peggy. I asked her if she would come to the beach after work, but she said she couldn't. Even though Pam spent almost every weekend helping me with the dogs, birthdays were sacred for her. Plus, sometimes the events at the beach were too depressing for her to face.

I stayed at the beach until five o'clock, stealing every last moment to fuss over Peggy and her pups until I had to go home and shower before Pam arrived. My heart was heavy and I just wasn't into celebrating. When I reached the house, I drank an overpoured shot of scotch to take the edge off my shattered nerves before getting into the shower in hopes of washing away my day.

I took Pam out to dinner at a French restaurant in Palmas del Mar. I tried not to talk about Peggy, but that left me without words. I'm typically a man who has a lot to say, so it was obvious I was struggling. I felt sad that, once again, Pam and her needs were being pushed to the back burner. I hated myself for doing it.

After hearing about Peggy that afternoon, Pam had spontaneously booked a trip for the two of us to Saint Thomas, leaving Puerto Rico the day after Christmas. During the course of our marriage, it had often been like pulling teeth to get her to try my extreme sports, so she thought it would be a great surprise for me to get our open water certification in scuba diving. Normally I would have jumped at the opportunity, but after three months of living in

Puerto Rico, I'd started to lose interest in things that used to be at the center of my life.

"C'mon, we'll get certified, spend some time together, just you and me."

"Who's going to watch the dogs?"

"You can't be responsible for them every minute of every day, Steve. We need to get out of here, away from all this, recharge our batteries."

She was right. I needed to learn how to compartmentalize the events at the beach. The dogs were clearly beginning to take over my life and affect Pam's.

I finally relented.

Early the next morning, Pam joined me at the beach. Peggy quietly greeted us; she seemed understandably worried and sad. She sighed as she soaked in our comforting caresses. I distracted her while Pam carefully extracted the injured puppy from her litter. She held him in a soft towel and, along with Sandra, we drove to a nearby horse farmer Sandra knew, hoping to get the pup some medical attention.

When we arrived, Sandra explained to the farmer in Spanish what had happened.

The farmer peeked inside the towel and shook his head, his expression grim. Sandra pleaded.

The farmer finally gave in. He reset the shattered bone as best he could, then stitched up the gash in the pup's skin where the bone had torn through. Although we tried our best to comfort the little dog, he whimpered and yelped in pain. Pam and I cried because we knew this wasn't a real fix. The puppy's bone was still severely broken, and there was nothing we could do about that. And although the care we gave would prolong his life, I knew it wasn't going to save him, and that broke my heart.

Back at the beach, Peggy sniffed at her sleeping pup's leg, then calmly allowed us to nestle the puppy against her chest. A few days earlier Peggy wouldn't come near us, but now she leaned her muzzle toward our hands so we could cuddle her face. I believe she knew we were trying to help her.

Later that day, Pam's growing concerns about my health were vindicated. I came down with a serious case of shingles that covered my back and left side. When I visited the doctor at Palmas del Mar, she exclaimed as soon as she met me, "You're the guy from the beach with the dogs." It seemed I was gaining a reputation. She noted that shingles are often sparked by "extreme emotional stress."

Just like mange in dogs, I thought.

I was not going to let it interfere with our trip, partly because of my commitment to Pam but also because I obviously needed to relieve my stress. We headed to Saint Thomas for our diving lessons on December 26. As the small plane took off from San Juan and headed over the eastern side of the island, I felt like a neglectful father leaving his children in need. I didn't talk the entire flight.

The first few days, I was too embarrassed about the hideous rash covering my body to let go and enjoy myself. Even on vacation, I felt like a leper.

But by the end of the week, I started to feel like my old self.

"Hey, Pammie, why don't we come back here every month? It's not far. We could totally do this!"

But when we got back to our lives in Puerto Rico, I resumed sliding downhill.

Since the event with her puppies, Peggy never let me out of her sight. She followed me around the beach while I did my rounds. She needed to know where I was all the time. She proudly showed me her puppies every day, allowing me to pick them up and enjoy them with her. She savored my contact, always breathing a sigh of relief at my touch.

But, as with so many of these dogs' stories, our interventions only went so far. A few months after we rescued Peggy's litter, Peggy wandered away from the pack and me during the morning feeding. Suddenly I heard a screech of car tires on the road. I was filled with dread. I ran toward the sound and found Peggy lying limp on the side of the road. I would bury another friend that day.

ELEVEN

I still ran into Carlos and Dominga, the old fisherman and his wife, from time to time, and they never failed to warn me to be careful. But one morning, their tone was different.

"There are men looking for you, asking a lot of questions: when you come to the beach, where you park, if you're alone."

"Really? What else do they say?" I asked the couple.

They shook their heads in unison. "We don't want to get involved, Stephen. It's not safe." I knew they were concerned for my safety, but fearful about their own as well, so I didn't push the issue.

"Thank you for warning me," I said. "It'll be okay, I promise."

"Keep your eyes open, *mi hijo*. The men driving Yabucoa municipal cars and the pickup trucks from the refinery up the road are asking about you. So are the people from the hotel down the other end of the beach. You gotta watch your back."

Dominga gave me a hug and Carlos offered a steely handshake before they walked off to fish for their food for the week.

I walked the beach with my pack, my thoughts consumed with what they'd told me. For the past few weeks, I'd had a bad feeling I was being watched. Now my suspicions were confirmed. It was reassuring to know I hadn't become totally paranoid, but this meant that there were in fact strange men tracking my movements. Quite frankly, I think I'd have preferred paranoia.

Heeding the warning—in my own way—I started carrying a billy club and a machete on my belt when I went to the beach. I was worried not just about myself, but about what this meant for my dogs. At least I had a better idea who was watching now.

Or I thought I did.

The area of the beach where I spent my days with the dogs may have been remote, but Playa Lucia is also home to a couple of resort hotels. One day I wandered off my stretch of sand toward the hotels, looking for a few of the dogs that had gone missing a few days before. As I poked around, three hotel employees wielding machetes approached me.

They said something to me in Spanish, and I made out a few phrases: "You're on private property, man. . . . You need to leave."

Taking the nice-guy approach, I responded, in English, "No worries, bro. I've just gotta find my dogs and I'll be on my way." I smiled and gave them a polite wave.

Then they shouted something at me. I had no idea what the words meant, but given the irate tone of their voices, confrontational body language, and raised machetes, I was pretty sure they weren't offering to buy me a drink at the poolside bar.

I've always believed you shouldn't escalate a situation by drawing a weapon except when you plan to use it, but I was quickly formulating a plan of attack if things went bad. It was one machete against three.

With my hands in front of me, palms facing them to communicate that I wasn't a threat, I asked politely, "Do any of you speak English?"

"A little," one of the men said.

"I don't want any trouble, man. I'm just taking care of some sick dogs over at the old boathouse a mile up the beach, and a couple of them wandered off."

The man's expression softened. He turned to the others and translated what I said. They lowered their machetes.

"Have you seen my dogs?"

The English speaker nodded. "Dead." He pointed to an area at the edge of the jungle with his leathery hand. "Over there."

I knew not to ask who did it, or how. The uncomfortable expressions on their faces said it all.

The men were looking over their shoulders, as though they feared getting in trouble for talking to me.

"A local hotel is trying to make the beach more beautiful for visitors. They told us to kill any stray dog on the beach and stop anyone from feeding them." He paused. "Including you."

"Really? The hotel owners know about me?"

"They want you to stay away. Or else."

"Or else what?"

He didn't answer. He wasn't trying to threaten me as he had at the start of the confrontation. And while I appreciated that they were cutting me some slack, I also knew they meant business and I needed to be more careful about venturing to this part of the beach.

"Can I please get the dogs so I can give them a proper burial?"

They looked anxious and talked among themselves for a minute.

"Make it fast."

When I returned with my truck twenty minutes later, the men were waiting next to the dogs. The smell of decay coming off the corpses was sickening. They'd covered their noses with their bandannas to ward off the stench. Sadly, I had become accustomed to it.

The men watched as I struggled to roll the dogs into the sheets I'd brought and put them in the plastic storage bins in the back of my truck. It was the only sanitary way to transport them. After I'd moved a couple of the dogs on my own, the men stepped in to help.

"Thank you," I said to them. I felt a little light-headed. It was a bit surreal to express gratitude to the very men who had committed such a violent act.

As I got in the truck to leave, I glanced back at the sanitation men. They were all staring at their feet. I had a feeling—or perhaps just a hope—that this was because they felt ashamed.

TWELVE

In the weeks that followed, more and more dogs disappeared from the beach. I started slowly driving the entire length of the long road to the beach, combing for remains. The stench of death along that route became overwhelming. I started finding dead dogs stuffed into plastic bags, crammed into five-gallon pails, and thrown into the ditch on the side of the road. Some appeared to have been poisoned, others beaten to death.

The attacks were escalating—in frequency and brutality. I couldn't continue to just clean up the mess without doing anything about it. It was time for another visit to the police station to see if I could finally persuade the authorities to step in.

"Local hotel owners are killing the dogs," I told the desk sergeant.

"How do you know?"

I didn't want to tell them about my encounter with the men on the beach a few days earlier. Nor did I want to rat out the fishermen who'd also told me the hotels were poisoning the dogs. It didn't matter anyway. The policeman behind the counter seemed pissed off that I was bothering him with such trivial matters.

Afterward, I decided to go over their heads: to the mayor's office. But even there, I got the same response: nothing.

So I continued to care for the survivors and newcomers to the pack—or, as I started calling it, perhaps a sign of my increasing preoccupation and obsession, "my pack." One day a young male German shepherd showed up. Not yet fully grown, he had the bravado of a teenager. He tried to mount all the females in my pack and challenge the already-established alpha males. I had to break up a few near battles before they escalated into something more serious that could result in injury.

Despite the troublemaking, it was obvious that this newcomer, whom I named Kyle, wanted to please me and that he had a lot of potential to be a great dog. Kyle had no food aggression, and even his roughhousing with the other males showed no killer tendencies. He was just trying in his clumsy young way to establish himself in the pack. When he wasn't causing mischief with the other dogs, he followed me around like he was glued to my knee. He just wanted to be near me all the time.

One morning while doing my rounds, I knelt down to pet some puppies while Kyle rubbed his face and shoulder against my side and nuzzled my face with his nose. It was a little obnoxious, but I ignored him as I focused on the little ones.

Next thing I knew, I felt warm liquid running down my lower back and into the waistband of my pants, right down my ass crack to the inside of my legs. I jumped up, startled, only to find Kyle with his leg still hoisted, finishing his pee. He looked at me with an expression that closely resembled a smile. He was marking his territory: me.

Pissed off and grossed out at the same time, I started to strip off my pants and shirt. I got my pants down as far as my ankles before they stuck on my boots. Fortunately, no one was passing by at that moment, as I'm sure it was quite a sight. After I got them off, I walked back to the truck for a change of clothes. Kyle pranced along beside me like nothing had happened.

I slipped into my surf shorts, grabbed a towel, and made for the shoreline to take a swim, sixty dogs in tow. It seemed a good opportunity to do some training with Kyle: He'd given me a bath, now I was going to give him one. He took it like a trooper, sitting quietly, ears down, sulking between my knees in the shallow water while I bathed him. As I did with all the dogs over time to kick-start the healing process for their skin, I used medicated shampoo and rinsed it with fresh water. Often, the dogs' coats would start to grow again soon afterward.

I don't know what it was about sitting in the ocean with Kyle that day, but his disposition changed toward both the pack and me. From that day on, he fit in like he'd been there all along.

The next afternoon, in the midst of a drenching rain, two Texans in one of the oil refinery pickup trucks pulled alongside me when I was feeding the dogs. The refinery was about two miles up the road, and I was accustomed to seeing these trucks trolling the beach from time to time, the occupants checking me out. Usually the trucks made the dogs a bit jumpy, but they didn't seem bothered this time.

The passenger in the pickup rolled down his window.

"Hey, what's up?" I said without looking up from what I was doing with the dogs. I wasn't sure what these guys wanted, and they didn't look threatening, but I didn't feel much like talking.

"We've been hearing about this long-haired dog guy at the beach, so we wanted to check it out for ourselves. You're kind of a legend back at the plant."

When I stopped and looked up, they were both smiling down at the dogs. The driver shut off the engine, and they got out, despite the rain. The dogs nosed at their hands, and the guys leaned down to give a few of them a pat.

"This is amazing, all these dogs are really dialed into you. I'm really impressed, my friend."

The dogs were behaving like they knew these guys were friends. If the dogs felt that way, they must be all right.

"Hey, I'm Stephen," I said, extending a hand to shake. They introduced themselves, and we took shelter under a palm tree.

"You seem like a nice guy, but you're sure pissing some people off, you know. They don't like the bad rap this area's getting."

"All I'm doing is taking care of a bunch of stray dogs."

"You've drawn a lot of negative publicity to this area, and people don't like that much. It's bad for business." The driver had a concerned look on his face when he spoke. I knew he was probably right.

"Maybe if these businesspeople spent some of their time and money helping with the problem instead of just bitching about it, the problem wouldn't exist, and I wouldn't have to clean up somebody else's mess. Why don't you take that message back to them?"

"Look, I hear you. I'm on your side, but, seriously, watch yourself, okay? I envy your heart and tenacity coming down here every day, but, like I said, some people want you to go away, you know what I mean?"

Jesus, the warnings were coming from all directions now.

One of the men gestured at the machete and billy club on my hip. "Is that all you have for protection?"

"Yep."

"I'd consider getting a sidearm, if I were you."

"Thanks, but no offense, I hate guns."

"How much you shelling out for all this dog food, man? This can't be cheap."

"Upward of a thousand a month. It's cutting into my and my wife's savings pretty seriously, to be honest."

"Damn." They both reached for their wallets, pulled out some cash, and handed it to me. "You're doing a good thing here, brother."

I'm not sure what these men expected when they arrived, having heard only what a nuisance the dog guy was, but I got the sense they left with an understanding that I was a decent guy who was just trying to do right by these defenseless animals. It was a comfort to know there were still sympathetic folks out there. But they were few and far between.

THIRTEEN

fter the Texans left the area, I took another walk down the beach toward the hotels. Seventy or so dogs trailed along behind me.

As I drew near a building that had once enclosed an abandoned public swimming pool, several men approached me from the edge of the jungle. They were gardeners for a local hotel, tasked with cropping the palm trees and removing coconuts so people didn't get clobbered by one while walking the beach (an experience I could relate to). As I neared them, the dogs moved in front of me and started to growl, as if trying to keep them away from me. Some of the dogs had been with me for only a few days or weeks. Their loyalty impressed me and emboldened me.

Feeling safer with them at my side, I stepped in front of the pack and quieted them so I could speak to the men, who kept looking over their shoulders and acting a little nervous. I got the sense, as with the men I'd encountered before, that they didn't want to be seen fraternizing with the enemy.

"The owners are furious with you, man. You shouldn't have gone to the police and the mayor's office. They don't like that."

Turns out I was wrong about the police doing nothing. After I left the station the last time, they evidently went straight to the hotel owners with my complaint about the dog killings.

Another worker put his hand on my shoulder, a grave look on his face. "People talk to you, but you don't listen. You must listen this time: Bad things can happen here. It's not just the dogs that go missing. You can too."

I could feel my adrenaline pumping. It wasn't fear, but anger: I couldn't just walk away and let evil win here. But as much as I wanted these guys, who seemed to mean well, to tell their bosses that I wouldn't back down, I knew they couldn't pass along a message from me without putting themselves at risk.

"I really appreciate your telling me," I said, taking a deep breath and trying to keep my cool. "Will you please let me know if you hear something is coming down that I need to know about?"

I shook their hands good-bye and walked back to the boathouse, lost in thought. *Holy shit. How did I go from feeding dogs to having my life threatened?*

Instead of stopping, like a normal person might have, I grew more determined. I'd never been particularly good at walking away from bullies. I never would have imagined that animal rescue would become the most extreme sport in my life.

Unable to give the sickest dogs the level of medical care they needed, I looked up every veterinary clinic I could find on the island. One afternoon I made a visit to the nearest one, hoping I could enlist their help. I didn't even make it past the woman at the front desk.

"Do not bring those street dogs anywhere near this practice! We have a clientele to think of. We are not equipped to do anything with *satos,* only personal pets."

In the meantime, I started seeing more refinery trucks and municipal cars parking in the near distance on the beach road and then just sitting there, presumably watching me. My suspicions became fact when I saw them taking pictures through their windows of the pack and me. When I tried to approach them, they sped away as soon as they realized they'd been seen.

This happened several times, until one morning they grew a little bolder. When I was walking the jungle trails, doing my rounds, I heard someone or something following me a short distance behind. Was it one of my dogs? An iguana?

I didn't think so.

I dropped the buckets of food and water I was carrying, grabbed my machete from my belt, and quickly circled back the way I'd come, hoping to catch the people who were tracking me and find out what they were doing. With my pack at my side, it was hard to be stealthy, so the element of surprise was not with me, but the safety of numbers was. When I reached the spot where I figured the men would be, I heard a car start, doors slam shut, and the sound of spinning tires spitting gravel as they pulled away. As the car receded up the road, I noticed that it was yet another municipal vehicle.

Someone was clearly sending me a message. I felt like I'd opened Pandora's box the day I discovered the dogs at the beach. It was becoming more and more obvious that I was in over my head. And my dogs were going to keep dying.

FOURTEEN

am and I had been telling our friends Yann and Laurence about the
dogs for months, so when they arrived from France for a visit in Feb-
ruary, they were curious to see the pack for themselves. I'm sure that
like most people back home I'd told about the dogs, they thought I was exag-
gerating. I needed people like Yann and Laurence to see what was happening
firsthand, so maybe they could help spread the word and I could make a real
difference.

The four of us headed to the beach in the morning for the breakfast feeding. I had offered to go early on my own, so they could sleep in, but they
insisted that they wanted to go too and that I keep to my schedule.

As I drove down the long approach road to the beach, they conversed
with each other in French. Laurence sounded concerned, so I adjusted my
rearview mirror to make eye contact with Yann.

"What's up, dude? You guys okay?" I asked.

"Man, it's so isolated."

"I think that's why people are able to get away with the horrible things they do here."

As we got close to the beach, I rolled down the window and gave my signature coqui whistle to get the dogs' attention. Within moments, some fifty of them were following the truck. Yann and Laurence unbuckled their seat belts and turned around to kneel on the backseat so they could see the pack trailing behind us.

"Wow, look how they come for you!" Yann said.

Laurence had tears in her eyes. "They're so skinny."

I knew she'd struggle when she met the dogs for the first time, as Pam had. But she was soon overcome by the need to give them love and asked me to stop to let her out. Not exactly what I thought would happen, but I was happy to see her embrace my pack. Much of the morning, Pam and Laurence sat in the sand near the water's edge with the majority of the pack around them. A few people I had taken to the beach in the past had been afraid to touch them because of their mange, but, like Pam, Laurence didn't care. She was able to see past the dogs' horrible condition and love them anyway. Yann and I watched from a distance, laughing to ourselves at the sight of our usually well-dressed and coiffed wives parked in the midst of what seemed like the mangiest, skinniest, most beat-up dogs anyone ever laid eyes on. Our wives appeared to be in heaven. Even the dogs that were normally afraid of their own shadows got in on the action, getting love from the gals.

When the women got up to take a walk, I showed Yann around the beach: where I fed the dogs, the burial ground, and where the dogs hid in the jungle. Several of the alpha dogs, which rarely left my side when I was there, followed us. When we got the boathouse, I gestured with my finger across my lips to Yann.

"Look," I whispered, pointing across the boat slip.

Pam and Laurence had gotten there ahead of us and were now sitting cross-legged on the glass-covered concrete floor with one of the wariest dogs I'd encountered so far. I called him Sheppie, and he'd never let me touch him.

"This is amazing," I said.

For five months, Sheppie had been schlepping around behind me wherever I went—he was part of the original crew I'd met in October—but he'd been too scared for human contact. Now he was nuzzling Laurence's neck and lying on his back for belly rubs.

An unexpected feeling came over me: a vague, slight jealousy. That's how attached to these dogs I'd gotten. Sheppie was my boy, and I wanted in on the action. Yann and I approached slowly. Sheppie lay still as I put my hand on his side. I could feel his heart racing. So was mine. And then I felt his body relax under my caress. He turned to face me with his head down and placed his head in my lap. He sighed and rolled over on his back so I could pet his belly too. He was mine now—or, more accurately, ours.

One day during their visit, Laurence, Yann, and I decided to head up to Arecibo on the north central coast of the island to do a little sightseeing and explore the beautiful beaches while Pam was at work. Pam and I had been there a few times before and thought it was beautiful. Unfortunately, that wasn't our experience there this time around: it was at Arecibo where I finally hit the breaking point.

I parked the truck at an old abandoned restaurant east of the main village. It was a pretty rural area and the old road was overgrown with jungle foliage. The houses were rundown and in disrepair, but the community was fairly quiet, so we weren't too concerned about anyone breaking into the truck. We grabbed only what we needed, knowing we'd be close enough to come back if we had forgotten anything. I locked the truck and we hightailed it to the beach.

Yann and I went snorkeling while Laurence caught some rays. Floating facedown in the warm Caribbean water with my snorkel and my mask, I felt truly relaxed for the first time since we'd moved to Puerto Rico. Suddenly I was yanked out of my reverie by the sound of Yann shouting and plowing through waist-deep water, frantically trying to get back to shore. I glanced over in that direction in time to see three men running away, their arms loaded with our stuff. I jumped up and was right behind Yann heading for the shore.

Yann and I looked at each other and, without words, we started chasing the thieves down the beach. I was a little faster and managed to gain some ground. One of them broke left and plowed through the jungle toward the main road. The other two kept running. I glanced back to see Yann chase the guy into the jungle. When I turned back, the two clowns in front of me broke left and headed into the jungle too. I was able to follow the trail of smashed grass and ended up in someone's backyard. As I exited the property through a fallen gate, I saw a heavy metal pipe, about three feet long. I grabbed it as I ran. Until that moment, I hadn't given a lot of thought to what the hell I was going to do if I actually caught these guys.

A few seconds later, I popped out onto a narrow paved road in front of the house. I heard the slapping of bare feet on the asphalt to my left and to my right. I chose right, figuring maybe they were headed back to town. I ran until I had nothing left, then stopped and caught my breath, wondering what the hell to do next. I turned and jogged back in the direction of the truck.

That's when I heard the laughter and voices mocking me in English. They were coming from a house on my right.

I slowed to a walk until I came to the edge of the driveway. I stopped and stared at the men. They sat silently but for a little mumbling among themselves.

One of the men stood up and put his hands in the air over his head. He said something in Spanish. I didn't understand the words, but I knew he was challenging me.

I stood my ground and stared back at him. The pipe at my side was visible. I'm pretty sure it was the only reason they didn't come closer. But I was alone, barefoot, in nothing but a pair of surf shorts.

How dumb is this?

I started to walk away, knowing I couldn't do anything but get myself killed. The adrenaline started to ebb. My feet were killing me. I was pissed. I swung the pipe like a baseball bat at branches alongside the road as I walked the walk of shame back to the truck.

I found Yann standing next to Laurence on the side of the road next to the truck. He had a pipe too.

Yann and Laurence had knocked on a few doors until they found someone willing to let them phone the police. We waited by the truck, which was fortunately still there, for over an hour. But no one showed up.

"Should we go try to get our stuff back?" Yann asked. I think we both knew the thieves had no incentive to give anything back easily, but we had to give it a shot.

We walked back to the house without any exchange of words and took up positions at the end of the driveway.

"We just want our stuff, man," I shouted to the guys at the house. "No trouble, just our stuff, okay?"

They laughed.

I looked at Yann. "I guess we're done negotiating then." I knew they had understood what I'd said since they'd been mocking me in English a few minutes earlier.

Yann and I nodded at each other and headed down the driveway. This is exactly what Pam had been worried about after my snorkeling experience with Brandon. She was right: I'd finally reached the point where I wouldn't take the sensible route and walk away from danger.

The shocked expressions on the faces of the men at the house betrayed their fear. They were *not* expecting this. A couple of them popped up from where they were sitting and backed away.

"Come on, guys, just give us back our things. We want to go home," I said in an eerily calm voice.

Nothing.

I had seen a couple of machetes leaning against the wall they'd been sitting on, but no one made a move toward them.

"I'm not leaving without my shit!" I said.

One of the men made a quick grab for the machete next to his leg, and, as he drew back, Yann and I countered by swinging our pipes in his direction, knocking the machete out of his hand. The man stumbled back, tripping on a tree stump, and fell to his side.

The rest of the crew started screaming at us in Spanish. A couple of them reached for the remaining machetes, but no one moved toward us. I was steely on the outside, but inside I was shitting bricks. I knew Yann felt the same.

"Fuck this, man," I whispered to Yann. "It's not worth getting killed for. Let's go."

We slowly backed up until we were sure we were out of reach.

"How the hell are we going to get home, dude?" Yann asked. The thieves had the keys to the truck, as well as Yann and Laurence's wallets and cell phones. My phone and wallet were still hidden inside the truck. Wearing only our surf shorts and no shoes, we started to feel a chill as the day grew short. We needed to do something soon.

A young man we'd seen fishing earlier in the day came walking up the road. We were able to borrow his cell phone to call Pam and ask her to get someone at her company to help. I was hoping that someone could bring us the spare truck key.

I tried Pam's cell but it kept going to voice mail. I didn't want to leave the truck there, because I knew these assholes would steal it as soon as we left. For a moment I thought about busting one of the truck's windows, but there was no spare key inside, so what was the point?

We were standing in the last of the remaining sunlight at the edge of a rundown property next to our useless truck, when a police car cruised by. We ran to the edge of the road to flag it down. Miraculously, the car made a U-turn and slowly drove back to where we stood.

"Do you speak English?" I asked the cop when he pulled up. He did. So we told him what had happened to our stuff, the confrontation in the yard.

"Yeah, I know, I already heard all about it. A neighbor called a while ago, said a couple of crazy gringos with pipes were in the neighborhood threatening people."

"Really? So why didn't you come then?"

"I figured you must be gone by now, so why bother?"

I wasn't too surprised by his who-gives-a-shit attitude, but Yann and Laurence were visibly upset.

"Why don't you head back to your fancy resort instead of hanging out here?" the cop said. "It's not safe around here for you after what you did."

"Excuse me? Not sure if you understand what happened here, but we were the ones who were robbed! Not the other way around."

"You should go home now. Seriously."

"We'd love to leave but those men have our keys!"

The cop took a step toward me. "You need to calm down. I'll go talk to those men and see if I can get your keys back."

"Fine, I'll calm down, but we're coming with you."

Back up the road, the cop greeted the men at the house like old friends. There were handshakes and hugs all around. There was a friendly conversation in Spanish punctuated by laughter.

Meanwhile, a couple of women emerged on an upstairs balcony. They pointed toward the cinder-block wall where the men had been sitting earlier. It seemed to me they were trying to tell us there was something behind that wall. *"I'm sorry,"* they mouthed.

The cop came back up the driveway. "They don't know anything about your stuff."

I pointed to a tall skinny kid standing with the group. "He's wearing my shirt." It had MEC printed in bold yellow letters on the front.

"So? No way to prove that's yours."

"Where did you get that shirt, bro?" I yelled to the kid.

"Surf shop!" the cop answered for him.

I was dumbstruck.

"Sir, you need to get back to your truck."

"And what do you suggest we do when we get back to the truck? They have our damn keys!"

The cop pulled me to the side and whispered, "Listen, I want to help you. I grew up in this community, and I know these people. I can get your keys back, but they don't have anything else of yours. You understand?"

I could not believe the police tactics I was witnessing. What choice did we have but to follow his lead?

"Go ahead. I just want to get the hell out of here," I said.

A few minutes later, the cop turned up with our duffel bag, the very one that had been swiped from the beach. Inside were the keys to the truck. And nothing else.

I guess I was supposed to be grateful.

"I'd like to file a police report for my insurance company," I told him.

"I'm sorry, sir. I can't do that. It's late, and I need to be getting back."

I wasn't taking no for an answer anymore, and followed him back to his cruiser where his yet unseen partner was in the front passenger seat. As he was getting in and shutting the door, another police car pulled up behind him. We'd been dealing with the municipal cops up until now, but this one was marked Policia de Puerto Rico.

"Is everything all right?"

"Actually, no, it's not, officer."

The municipal cop jumped back out of his car like a shot. Inside the car, his partner was scribbling something on a piece of paper. When she was done, she handed it to our guy, who handed it to me. "Your report. You can go home now."

I looked down at the piece of paper he handed me. Our official police report was written on Hello Kitty stationery.

CHAPTER FIFTEEN

The day after the robbery in Arecibo, everybody was on edge. No one more than me.

"Stephen, I think you're losing your grip," Pam said that morning during the drive to her office. "You lose your keys, and you go ballistic. You used to choose your battles wisely, but these days you don't seem to be afraid of anyone or anything. You took those guys on even though you were totally outnumbered. The old you would never have done that. I'm afraid it's going to get you killed."

"It wasn't as simple as losing my fucking keys!"

"Steve, you know what I mean."

"Give it a rest!" I snapped, although somewhere deep in my subconscious what remained of my reason knew she was right.

"Stephen, I love you, but this isn't like you. Please, don't bite my head off."

This was becoming a common theme in our conversation: Pam worrying, me being obstinate.

She kissed me good-bye. "Please be safe." The look of concern in her eyes killed me. I hated that I was making her feel this way. She didn't deserve it.

I mumbled something back to her as she shut the door (this had also become a standard bit of behavior on my part). As I made a U-turn to exit the facility, I saw her wave to me in my peripheral vision. I didn't bother to wave back.

I knew my life was spiraling out of control. I knew she was right, I was losing my grip on reality, getting entirely consumed by the beach and my quest to save the dogs. I didn't even have a plan or a solution in place. I just knew I had to do something, because if I didn't, no one else would. I knew that the other people helping the dogs shared some compassion and food with them, but they'd given up on the possibility of actually saving the dogs and stopping the cycle of abuse.

But it wasn't right to take out my frustration on Pam. I didn't want to turn into one of those people who loves animals but hates human beings. I resolved to call Pam later to apologize.

I'm pretty sure I never did.

In order to get some much-needed relaxation in, after we fed the dogs Yann and I decided to hang out on the beach at Palmas del Mar and do some snorkeling instead of going elsewhere.

There was a coral reef in the bay that created a natural wave break. It wasn't ideal for snorkeling, but the water was clean and clear, and we had a great time swimming. I hadn't brought my swim fins with me, and after an hour or so my legs were starting to get tired. I turned to head back to shore.

I felt something brush against my lower back and the back of my arm. I gasped, sucking in water through my snorkel. I pulled my face out of the water, panicked. Whatever had just rubbed up against me was really big.

"Yann!"

He was by my side in a flash. "What's wrong?"

"Something huge just bumped me, bro." He could tell by the look on my face that I wasn't kidding around.

We looked around in the water, but whatever it was had stirred up the sand, and the water was cloudy now. We couldn't see anything.

"Should we make a break for shore?"

"Hey, we only need to be faster than the slowest guy," he joked. Yann swam better and faster than anyone I knew.

"That's comforting. Thanks!"

Suddenly the smile on his face evaporated. "Dude, it just brushed against me!" he shouted.

And then it brushed against both of us at the same time, which was intense since we were several feet apart.

"What the—"

Right between us, the water broke, and an enormous manatee surfaced. The shock initially scared us, but then we started laughing. The manatee blew her big blubbery nose in my face.

"I wonder how long she was checking us out," Yann said.

"She must have been watching us this whole time, and finally summoned the courage to come over and play."

She was soft to the touch and remarkably gentle with us. We put our arms out to the sides and she swam between us, making contact with both of us as she passed.

Two smaller manatees surfaced a few feet away. They weren't as friendly and kept their distance.

"I bet those are her babies."

The mother stayed and swam with us for about an hour before she and her young ones went on their way. It was heaven.

CHAPTER SIXTEEN

After Yann and Laurence flew back to France, I returned to my solo routine with the dogs. One night, as I was lying in bed, I was woken in the wee hours of the morning by great claps of thunder and lightning that lit the room. The sound of rain pelting the windows and roof of the house was intense.

It was too late to go back to sleep and too early to start the day, so I lay still, careful not to wake Pam, waiting for my body to catch up to the business of my brain. Being tired didn't slow my thoughts anymore; it stirred them up, disrupting the balance of questions and answers. Everything was bothering me. We were running out of money to feed and care for the dogs. My life had become a constant struggle against attitudes: government, hotel owners, and even friends who worried about my safety. And it was driving a huge wedge between Pam and me.

My passion and concern for the dogs had set me apart from the rest of my species, it seemed, and I felt as alone and abandoned as the dogs. It wasn't enough to make me want to stop, but it was making me feel increasingly isolated, especially in those early hours of the morning when solutions are hardest to find. I was starting to feel more at home with the dogs on the beach than anywhere else. It was where I always wanted to be, but it wasn't mine, I didn't own it, and it was dangerous.

The following morning, I parked my truck near the metal storage containers by the boathouse. Kyle was the first one to greet me. "Hey, buddy, did you sleep okay?" I said as I knelt down to rub his ears and give him the affection he craved: the affection I'd come to realize that *I* craved as well.

However, the rest of the pack hadn't shown up yet. Usually, within moments of my arrival, I was surrounded by wagging tails and grinning faces nudging my legs and hands, but this morning was different. The dogs were slow to leave the safety of the jungle. Something was wrong. Maybe it was due to the storm the night before.

I filled the food bowls as the pack, which at this point numbered sixty-eight by my count, arrived hesitantly. They munched away on their breakfast but kept a close eye on me. Kera, a Jack Russell terrier, had recently given birth to a litter of five puppies, so I began loading up the two five-gallon pails I carried with supplies for them, as well as any other newcomers I might find along the way.

As I turned to walk across the parking lot toward a makeshift den Kera had made for her pups under a conveyer belt alongside the boathouse, the dogs abandoned their food and followed me closely. They knew my routine and rarely left the bowls until they'd finished eating. Now I was certain something was wrong.

I was about ten yards from the boathouse when I heard the first dogs growl. I followed their gaze to the open doorway on my right. Squinting into the sun, it was impossible to make anything out in that dark space. Slowly, my eyes began to adjust.

Uh-oh.

The silhouettes of two men facing my direction came into view. This couldn't be good. Ten different scenarios flooded my brain at the same time. I knew one thing for certain: They didn't usually hurt the dogs when I was around. At least not in plain sight. They had to be here for another reason.

I was aware of the dogs moving around me, but I didn't dare take my eyes off the men. They moved a few steps forward. One of them shouted something in Spanish and gestured for me to come over.

"No, gracias," I called out, waving as if to say good-bye.

They signaled again for me to come over, and took a few more steps in my direction. Behind them, more men appeared from the shadows. They wore sweat-stained wifebeater tank tops, and shirts pulled up over their heads and behind their necks.

I couldn't breathe. My heart was pounding in my ears and neck. Then I saw a reflection of light at their side. It confirmed what I dreaded the most: machetes.

"Aw, shit," I said to myself.

I'd been frozen in one spot, still holding the heavy buckets. I slowly bent my knees and lowered the buckets to the ground, while trying to judge the distance back to the truck without turning my head. I had left my machete and billy club inside. Pam was right: my judgment was starting to get cloudy.

As soon as my hands were free, the men took a few more steps out of the shadows. I felt my dogs lean into the threat. I hadn't realized until then that they'd moved ahead of me. *My* pack wasn't going to let this happen. I could feel an almost electric charge surging through them as they took up positions to fight. The other dogs flanked me, their mouths curled into snarls.

I debated my next move. I slowly drew the keys to the truck from my front pocket. It took incredible concentration to move my left foot, then my right as I began inching toward the vehicle. The dogs continued to stand guard. Any rivalry between the alpha dogs was set aside. They were teaming together, standing shoulder to shoulder, creating a boundary between me and the men. They never once glanced back at me looking for guidance. It was clear that they were taking control of the situation.

Everything seemed still and tense—the jungle, the attackers, the dogs, the ocean, time. The only thing moving was the air, which vibrated with deep, menacing growls.

I continued making small sidesteps toward the truck, keeping my eyes on the men as I went. The dogs followed my lead, taking small steps with me.

They were in full battle mode, ready to fight at any cost. I never took my eyes off the gang of men, looking for a signal or a sudden movement that indicated I should start running.

The dogs and I had only gained a short distance when the tension exploded, and the men made their move, breaking into a run toward me. I ran for the truck. The next few seconds seemed to pass in slow motion. I could hear my breathing, my shoes slapping against the gravel. A confused rush of sounds and images flooded my mind—shouting, barking, growling.

Then I heard a single sharp yelp and looked back to see Kyle fall in a heap on the ground. Instead of running away from the attackers, he and the other alphas ran toward the men to cut them off. Kyle was the fastest of the males. He must have gotten there first. He took a massive hit with a machete across his shoulder and deep into his rib cage. I saw him struggle to get up, but he couldn't. The sounds of his yelps of pain mixed with the hollow thuds of metal pipes hitting flesh and bone. I could do nothing to help him.

I reached the truck, the rest of my escorts still surrounding me. Not one dog had abandoned me. They'd either defended or attacked.

Tears and sweat stained my shirt as I fumbled with my keys to start the vehicle, then laid on the horn. The moment the dogs heard the honk and the sound of the engine, they vanished into the jungle.

The men stopped and looked in my direction. I looked through the windshield at the carnage. My eyes stung with sweat and tears.

Dogs lay dead in the gravel ten yards away. Two of them were still moving, but dying fast.

I gripped the wheel and stared at the butchers. I felt more rage than I knew what to do with. These savages had just killed my dogs, whose trust and love I'd worked so hard to earn. I couldn't let them get away with this.

I put the truck in gear. If I gunned it now, I could mow them down before they reached the boathouse. I could end this.

I shook my head clear and watched the men disappear back into the shadows from which they came.

"Cowards!"

It was quiet now except for the sound of the engine and the cold air-conditioning blowing through the vents. I gripped the wheel to stop my hands from shaking. I wondered whether to stay or go. If I got out of the truck and the men came back, then my dogs had died in vain. They gave their lives to save mine, and my head was spinning trying to make sense of what the hell just happened.

I drove the long road from the beach back to civilization. I wasn't afraid anymore, just angry and more hurt than I could have ever imagined.

Out of sheer desperation, I went to the police station. Did I really expect anything would be different this time? Isn't that how they describe insanity: doing the same thing over and over and expecting a different result?

I hoped that this time, when there was a human being threatened instead of a dog, I'd get a different reaction. I was sure that killing island visitors was much worse for tourism than killing stray dogs on the beach. However, the policeman at the counter only shrugged his shoulders.

"What do you want me to do?"

"Your job! Or is that too much to ask?"

"Maybe you don't belong here. You should go home before someone gets hurt."

The combination of the smart-ass grin he wore and the sarcastic tone in his voice made it obvious I was getting nowhere, so I left the station before I said something I'd likely regret. After my pointless visit to the police, I called Pam to tell her what happened.

"Please don't go back, hon," she pleaded. "Enough is enough! I don't want to lose you. Not to this."

I called my brother Barry, who said the same thing.

After talking to them both, I sat in my truck in the middle of town. I felt confused and slightly disoriented. My enemies, whoever they were, they weren't just threatening me anymore. They were actually taking action against me. Was the right to abuse animals so important that they would have killed me?

Finally, I had to go back to the beach, to my friends. Real friends don't run away; they support each other. I had only witnessed Kyle being wounded, but as I had driven away there were others on the ground. Maybe they were still alive. Maybe I could save them. At the very least, I wanted to bury my friends before nightfall. I owed them that.

Despite Pam and my brother's warnings, I couldn't get there fast enough.

Back at the beach, I walked over to the dogs. Kyle was hacked clean through. Two others were also gone.

I dug graves for them. And then, one by one, I carried these heroes to their final resting place. The dogs, including a couple that had been injured in the fight, filtered out of the jungle and fell in behind me as if to pay their respects. My dogs had chosen to die so I could live. They could have run, but they stayed to protect me. They died as dogs, not as discarded trash, destroyed by some pathetic drunk or a sick thug looking for entertainment. This had to be better. I needed it to be better.

My body went through the motions of burying them, but my brain shut down until the last grain of sand filled the final grave. When it was done, I collapsed, two words running through my head: *Now what?*

The body being buried could have just as easily been mine.

CHAPTER
SEVENTEEN

I tried the police one more time after the attack at the boathouse.

"I tell you already. Don't go there no more," the cop said.

"I'm burying two or three dogs a day, man. You've got to do something! Please!"

"It is illegal, what you are doing. You cannot bury any animal on the island without proper authorization. We could have you arrested."

They were going to arrest *me*? What was wrong with this place?

I felt like I was losing another piece of myself every time I buried another dog. If I didn't do something drastic, nothing would ever change for them. In the meantime, Pam and I were fighting more and more the further down this spiral I traveled. She was watching the man she loved drown in a cause that was likely going to kill him.

I also put her job at risk after a run-in with one of the security guards at her office one evening when I went to pick her up. They usually allowed me to drive inside the gates to spare her walking across the dark parking lot alone, but one night a new guard wouldn't let me in and I lost it. The guard reported me to the company for threatening him, and Pam was called in to speak to HR and her boss.

That night, she was furious. "It's like you can't control yourself anymore," she said over dinner.

"The guy was an asshole, Pam. He's lucky I didn't kick his ass."

"This is my job, Steve! You were out of line."

"All you care about is that damn job!"

"That job is our bread and butter, Steve! What do you think pays for all that dog food? For our house?"

She was completely right. The old me would have handled the situation differently.

I hung my head. "I'm sorry, Pammie. I don't know what's happening to me. I'm losing it. I can feel myself slipping further and further away."

She reached across the table for my hand. Her eyes filled with tears. "Steve," she said, her voice quiet now, "my biggest fear is that I'm going to get a call at my office one day telling me you're dead."

While she had accepted years earlier that she'd likely lose me to a climbing or flying accident, she never imagined it could be a homicide instead.

To save me, to save us, Pam decided to call in reinforcements. She still had contacts at a shelter in California where she'd volunteered years earlier, but they told her that they couldn't take dogs from Puerto Rico because of local rabies laws. After a little Internet research, she found a group called Save a Sato in San Juan. Save a Sato was founded in the midnineties by two women who had basically done what I was doing now—fed strays on the streets of San Juan. They teamed up and started a small animal shelter that had partnerships with a network of no-kill shelters in the States. Pam sent them an e-mail asking for advice or help.

She heard back from Betsy Freedman, Save a Sato's outreach coordinator, who was based in Boston. "Talk to Isabel Ramirez," she suggested. Isabel was a director at Save a Sato in San Juan. Pam and I felt hopeful for the first time in months.

Sadly, that hope didn't last long.

"I'm sorry, there's nothing we can do for you," Isabel told Pam when they spoke on the phone. "We've got our hands full here."

Clearly we were on our own.

Meanwhile, the situation was getting worse on the beach. A few times I saw what appeared to be locals, just regular guys hanging out with their families at the beach for the day, throwing food to the dogs. The dogs would grab the meat and run. Within minutes the dogs would be staggering like drunks until they fell down convulsing and died. A few times I was able to get the scraps before the dogs took them. I could see the beads of rat poison concealed inside the food.

Most weekends there were so many families that the dogs were always at risk of injury or worse. People would get angry when the dogs approached their barbecue pits and would shoo them away. Sometimes, at the end of the day, I'd find one or two dogs with half-eaten hot dogs in their mouths. The poison was so fast acting that they'd hit the ground dead before they could take a second bite.

During the week, it was the guys driving the refinery trucks I worried about. A couple of times I witnessed men jumping out of the trucks and pouring antifreeze into puddles of rainwater or the water dishes I'd set out for the dogs.

I was losing this battle, and I had nowhere to turn.

And then in April, Pam received an e-mail from a woman in Florida named Martha Sampson. She explained that she worked at the refinery several days every month, and that during her last trip to the island she'd noticed a new mom with her puppies by the main gate and was concerned for their welfare, so she contacted Isabel Ramirez, who then put her in touch with us.

She asked if we could help rescue the dogs and get them medical attention, and said that "maybe" she could find them a home.

What the hell was I going to do with the mom and her puppies even if I was able to capture them? The refinery plant's security guards weren't going to let me anywhere near the property. I had several dozen dogs of my own at the beach that needed better medical attention than I'd been able to provide. And even if we could afford to bring the dogs to a vet for treatment, the vets in the area had already made it pretty clear they wanted nothing to do with them.

I wasn't sure we'd be able to help Martha, considering we needed so much help ourselves.

"Martha's in town," Pam said one afternoon a few days later when she called me from her office. "She wants to meet you at the plant. Will you call her?" She gave me Martha's number. I didn't know what the hell I could do for her, but I dutifully called and we arranged to meet.

At the appointed time, I drove up to the main gate, but Martha wasn't there.

A couple of imposing security guards approached my truck. "This is private property. You need to leave now," one said in a way that didn't invite discussion.

"Please, I'm picking up an employee."

Just in time, a freckle-faced, auburn-haired woman came bouncing along in a bright orange jumpsuit. She had the kind of complexion that didn't fare well in the Puerto Rican sun. It had to be Martha.

"Jump in!" I said, pushing open the passenger door for her. My plan was to show her the dogs already in my care, so she would understand where I was coming from before she asked for any favors.

When we got to the beach, the sight of the dogs had her in tears. "I've been working with these dogs for months now," I explained to her." "I'm barely keeping them alive, and new strays turn up practically every day."

"What you're doing here is amazing, Stephen. I don't know how I could handle it."

"Caring about them isn't enough, though," I replied, hoping to enlist an ally to my cause. "There's an entire culture that needs to be changed. It's the people who dump them, the vets, the politicians, the businesspeople who ignore them and worse. To most of the locals, they're not even dogs, they're rats. The way the dogs beg for food is just an annoyance to them. Martha, I'm not making this up. Pam's coworkers, people who have lived here their whole lives, people who actually admire what I'm doing here, have told me that I'm fighting a losing battle. The only way to make a difference is to *do something*."

"Will you please come back to the plant and help me get that mother dog and her pups?"

Clearly she had her own cause. I appreciated her faith in me, but I couldn't take on another cause. I had to pick my battles.

"It won't be easy to do. A scared mother isn't going to want to be caught. And I don't know if you noticed, but the security guard wasn't too receptive when I arrived to pick you up. What makes you think they're going to let me help some stray dogs?"

"Can we please try?"

"What are you planning to do with the mother and the pups if we get them? Have you thought about that?"

She glanced at my pack nervously. "Can't we bring them down here?"

"Martha! You realize the locals call this place Dead Dog Beach, don't you?"

"I know, I know! But they'll kill her if she stays at the plant."

"They're probably going to kill her if she comes here. I lose dogs every day."

"Don't you think they have a better shot with you and your dogs?"

"Martha, my wife and I are already shelling out nearly a grand every month to feed these dogs. We're stretched pretty thin financially."

She smiled and nodded like she was listening to me, but I knew she wasn't.

"I'd like to get the dogs to a vet," she said in a singsong voice. I imagine she thought it would somehow sway me.

"Even if we were able to catch these dogs, there's no vet I know of who will take them. Do you know of someone who will? Maybe I missed one?"

Nope, nothing. She was full of hope and not much else.

As much as I was trying to resist Martha, I couldn't say no. I knew it from the moment I received her e-mail. These were innocent lives, and if I didn't do something about it, they faced certain death. I took Martha back to the plant to see what I could do.

Martha went in the gate herself and made her way to a rotting wooden foundation shielded by thick undergrowth where she thought the mother had made her den. She was only forty or fifty feet from where I stood on the outside of the fence. Watching her crawl through thick brush in her orange jumpsuit was a sight to see. She thrust her head into a narrow space between the foundation and the ground, then pulled out and yelled back at me, "I saw her for a second!"

"Forget it, Martha. It's not gonna happen now. You've scared her. She's going to move her pups all the way under the building. She has to want your help or you'll never get her. She'll just run, and I don't want her to abandon her pups."

Martha came back out, crying, her hands clenched. "She's all alone in there."

I asked Martha to stay by the truck for a few minutes. I walked over to the guards and asked if there was any way possible that they might let me in for a few minutes to get the dog and her pups. They wouldn't budge and insisted it was time for me to get in my truck and drive away

"I'm sorry it didn't turn out better, Martha. Sadly, I deal with this stuff daily, and there's nothing we can do right now."

"I feel so helpless, like I failed her," she said.

"I'll keep an eye out for her, okay? If she does relocate her pups outside the plant, I'll do everything in my power to get them to a safer place. It's the best I can do for now. The guards have pretty much tied my hands." I knew this wasn't the answer she'd hoped for.

I left Martha standing at the gate, tears still flowing down her cheeks. As I drove away, I felt bad. Not for Martha, but for the dogs.

CHAPTER EIGHTEEN

I was driving down the road to the beach one day in the spring when I turned the first corner after the long straightaway to find a car coming straight at me in my lane. The crazed driver had his head out the side window and was looking backward, so he didn't even notice he was driving in my lane. Over his screams and the wail of his horn, he couldn't hear me either. I swerved at the last minute, slammed on the brakes, and managed to avoid a collision.

As he passed by me (I admit it, I gave him the finger), I turned to see the reason why he was angry: There were two very large dogs staggering like drunks in the middle of the road. Their front legs were splayed in a wide stance as they braced themselves, trying not to fall over, but it wasn't working. First one would take a step, fall down, and struggle to get back up, then the other dog would do the same.

I pulled my truck diagonally across the middle of the road to block traffic until I could help the dogs make their way to the shoulder. Several cars pulled up to my roadblock, honking and shouting with indignation. I ignored them as I tried to help the two dogs. They were both so disoriented that I eventually picked them up one by one and carried them to the grass a few yards off the side of the road. They lay down and stayed there until I could move my truck out of the way of traffic. For the moment, they were safe.

In the few minutes I was gone, they hadn't budged. They were terribly skinny, and it was obvious they were deliriously ill. Up close, I could see that once upon a time they had been a full-bodied Rottweiler and a German shep-herd. I grabbed all the cans of wet food I had in the truck along with some water, and got them to eat and drink as much as they could handle. I waited with them a little while until they seemed more alert and coherent before I headed to the store for more food and dewormer.

When I returned, the two dogs were hiding in the bushes along the side of the road, as though waiting for me. The moment I pulled up, they greeted me with wagging tails and as much spring in their step as they were able to muster considering their physical condition. But within moments they were exhausted again, and I led them back to the edge of the jungle. I sat with them, hand-feeding them cans of wet food for about an hour before they fell asleep in my lap.

My heart was broken. I had seen some skinny, sick dogs in the last months at the beach, but not like this. I couldn't believe these dogs were still alive. The shepherd's skin draped off her bones in loose folds like wet paper towels over sticks. She had no muscle mass, only bone structure and mangy skin. The Rottweiler was in slightly better shape, but not by much. They both had collars hanging loosely around their necks. When I removed the collars, I noticed there were still a couple of links of broken chain dangling from them. They must have used the last of their strength to break free from the hell they were living in before they arrived here. And yet I thought they were strangely lucky, as this was the first time I didn't have to cut off a collar that had become deeply embedded in a dog's neck. Their starvation had likely spared them the long suffering of strangulation or serious infection I'd seen in so many of the dogs from whose flesh I'd had to cut out rusted bits of old restraints.

I certainly never planned to do veterinary work, but I was finding myself doing more and more of it by necessity. I'd seen some of the dogs die from the infections on their necks. And a few of the dogs that remained leery of humans wouldn't let me cut their collars off; I later found them dead.

As I left the two girls to attend to my regular rounds at the beach, I felt more depressed than I had in a while, and that was saying a lot. The girls tried to get in the truck with me, and I had to block them, which made me feel terrible. I opened another can of food and lured them back to the edge of the jungle, out of harm's way. Fortunately, the food held their interest long enough for me to slip away. It pained me to keep them separated from the rest of the pack, but I felt they'd be safer if they remained isolated until they gained enough strength to properly defend themselves if needed. The challenges a new dog faced trying to find its place within an already established pack were tough on the dog. They took a lot of energy and caused a lot of stress, both of which these girls couldn't afford at this time. They needed proper rest and nourishment in order to recover and become healthy again. I knew that as long as they had each other and remained hidden there alongside the isolated road they'd be okay, or at least I hoped so.

I did my rounds at the beach faster than usual, but I still spent several hours with the dogs. They had become so in tune with my moods, they knew I was feeling down and they tried everything in their power to make me feel better. I often struggled to believe that I was doing anything more than prolonging their inevitable death. I kept telling myself, if they died today, at least they had known that I loved them.

Later, on the way home from the beach, I stopped to look in on the girls again. They must have been in a deep sleep when I pulled up because they didn't hear the truck. It wasn't until I was right up on them that they startled awake. I had grabbed an old tarp that one of the fishermen had left at the beach, and used kite string that I kept in the truck to tie a rain shelter for them. Underneath, I lay a couple of blankets down to make a comfortable den where they could rest and regain their strength. They seemed grateful for my efforts. I soothed them back to sleep and sneaked back to the truck to make my way home. I didn't make it very far before I had to pull over and collect myself, I was crying so hard.

Over the next few days the girls seemed to be getting a bit stronger, and their spirits were improving, but they still had a long road to recovery. They seemed to enjoy my visits, and looked devastated when I left to tend to the other dogs. So I made it part of my routine to visit the girls on the way to the beach and again on the way home. I knew they still needed a little extra attention before they could be relocated to the beach with the others.

As the weekend neared, Pam was anxious to meet my newest friends. On Saturday morning, we were on our way to the beach bright and early. As I pulled up alongside the road near where I'd' made a den for the girls, I gave a whistle and a shout to summon them out of the jungle. On cue, they stumbled out of the foliage to greet me. As soon as they noticed Pam, it was love at first sight. They snuggled into her as if they'd found a long-lost friend. They tried to prance, but they were still too weak and emaciated to do much.

As I prepared their food, I looked back at Pam, who had the two girls pressed against her body as she sat on the concrete base of a utility pole at the side of the road. Pam tenderly wiped the goop from their eyes onto her pant leg. I knew this would be her reaction. Seeing these two beautiful creatures with so much love to offer, and yet so badly neglected and abused—how could you not feel devastated and helpless?

Lately I had been wondering if I was getting stronger or just desensitized to the carnage I witnessed daily. I refused to believe it was the latter. I never wanted to lose the ability to feel the dogs' pain. I'd rather feel the pain than feel nothing at all.

Pam and I needed to continue on to the beach to take care of the pack there before the weekend crowds started to arrive, putting the dogs in danger. Drunken people driving cars, motorcycles, and dune buggies made all the dogs vulnerable. Not to mention the poisoned food.

Not long after we set up for the morning feeding and meds at the storage containers, Sandra pulled up. The three of us fed the dogs together and talked for a bit.

"Have you been feeding the two big dogs up the road?" she asked. "I just went by there and saw they already had food and water. I figured it must be you."

I didn't know she'd been looking after them too. I usually knew when and where Sandra had been. I was used to finding leftover piles of kibble covered in ants. I knew she was struggling financially and doing the best she could for the dogs, but she typically fed the dogs one of the less expensive brands of dry dog food, and often the dogs wouldn't eat it. (Given how hungry these dogs were, goodness knows what was in the cheaper food.)

"I found them on the road a few days ago," I said. "They were in pretty bad shape."

"When I saw the bed, I thought maybe the owner had left it for them when he threw them away."

"Wishful thinking, Sandra. That was me."

"I've been calling the Rottweiler Nina, but I couldn't come up with a good name for the shepherd," she said. "Any thoughts?"

"She should have a good strong German name," Pam said. She had been traveling in Germany a lot for work over the last few years, so I wasn't surprised that she had an opinion. "There was a woman I used to work with in Biberach, Germany, named Nicole. She was a strong businesswoman but a really nice person. What about that?"

"I like it," Sandra and I said simultaneously.

So Nicole and Nina it was. Our sphere of care was expanding.

NINETEEN

Two months after we first heard from Isabel Ramirez, she sent Pam another e-mail reminding us that we were welcome to come volunteer with her organization in San Juan but insisting that we were not to contact any stateside shelters. I tried to feel sympathetic that she'd worked so hard to establish a pipeline to the States, but I was hurt and offended by her implication that we'd screw it up.

On top of that, after my initial experience with Martha and Isabel, Pam and I started receiving regular calls and e-mails from more and more people asking for help with dogs they'd seen while they were on the island for a family vacation. Turns out Isabel was sending them to me. I wanted her help, but instead I was getting her overflow work. My pack was between seventy and a hundred dogs at any given time now. Wasn't that enough?

Meanwhile, three new female dogs had started hanging around the beach, five little puppies fumbling around at their feet. One of the adult dogs in this group was a black Labrador, and judging by the coloring of the puppies and her engorged teats, she was the mom of the litter. All the dogs were skinny, and the pups were of an age when they'd need puppy food to supplement nursing.

Despite my best efforts, they were too scared of humans to let me get close enough to help them. They stayed in their own little pack on the perimeter of the beach, watching me interact with the rest of the dogs. I decided to call the Lab Lannie. There was no real reason for that particular name, I just liked the sound of it and it seemed to suit her. It was the first time I'd named a dog before handling it. The good news was that Lannie seemed to be a good mum to her pups, keeping a close eye on them. Puppies are naive, often with very little sense of fear. They had no idea that there were people out there who wanted to hurt or kill them. It gave me some comfort that the mother kept her babies out of reach of people at the beach.

But Lannie also looked tired, and I'm sure nursing was exhausting every bit of energy she had left. Strays who were mothers were at additional risk because they were torn between protecting their pups and saving their own lives. I'd seen it too many times, most brutally the morning I'd arrived at the tail end of some young men smashing a nursing mother to death because she'd growled at them when they tried to take her puppies. I'd chased the men away, dumbfounded why anyone would do such a thing. I suppose they thought they could make a few bucks selling the puppies. Occasionally some folks would grab one to take home to their kids. This might seem like they were saving the animals, but the pups were often too young to be taken from their mothers, or the people didn't understand the responsibility and expense of raising a puppy, so the puppy ended up right back where it started, but usually in much worse condition than when it was taken.

After several weeks of persistence, I'd finally gotten to know Lannie, the two other females, and the puppies, which were growing like little flowers. They were becoming quite a handful for Lannie to keep track of. And evidently they'd been watching me in action with the pack, because one morning they came waddling up to me and tried to climb my legs. They wanted to play with the other dogs. There weren't any other puppies at the beach then, so they were hanging on to some of the shorter dogs, pulling on their ears and pestering the older dogs until they'd get pissed off and growl or wander away to sulk under the metal storage containers.

Since puppies don't naturally know boundaries, they learn from their mothers as well as from the pack. It was beautiful to watch even the old seasoned veterans act stern yet playful with the pups. The three females seemed to let their guard down a little when they were in the presence of my pack. And the pack welcomed the new members without a hitch.

I continued to work on getting Lannie and the other two to trust me more. The key to their hearts was their puppies, so I would approach them only after the puppies had been climbing all over me. Between the scent of the pups and the other dogs rubbing their noses and sides all over me, it wasn't long before the three females let me pet their backs lightly and cuddle their faces. They were still apprehensive, but it was a breakthrough.

The following Saturday, Pam and I went to the beach early to beat the rush of visitors. We stayed with the dogs for a few hours, and then, in an effort to have some downtime together, headed off to San Juan for lunch and some leisurely sightseeing through the old fortified city. As the afternoon wore on, I got antsy about getting back to the dogs before nightfall. Checking in on them at the end of the day was a part of my daily routine. So after I dropped Pam at home, I went to the beach solo.

As was normal on weekends, the dogs were out of sorts, largely due to the chaos and commotion on the beach. It always made them anxious.

There were still a few people hanging out around the area, but most of the families had left. As I walked with my furry entourage, some people stopped to watch and waved. They were actually smiling. I was so proud of my dogs.

As I walked the sandy road in front of the boathouse looking for missing members of the pack to settle them down for the night, I could hear a lot of shouting and laughter coming from the far end of the parking area on the other side of the narrow strip of jungle palms. I picked up my pace to see what was happening, stopping at the edge of the jungle where I could watch without being seen.

There were two compact cars in the middle of the parking lot, their engines revving to a high-pitched screech. A couple of other cars were parked along the side of the lot, with men sitting on the hoods, watching the action.

Between the deafening roar of the revving engines and the men shouting, I heard barking coming from my left. It sounded frantic. I turned to see two men running out of the jungle near the edge of the boathouse, right where Lannie and the pups had made their den.

The men had all five of the whimpering puppies in their arms. I could tell these men weren't taking the puppies from the beach to make a few bucks selling them from a box on a street corner. These guys were out for blood.

Without a thought, I ran full speed toward them, leaping over the waist-high cinder-block wall like a runner over a hurdle. Upon landing, my left foot struck the trunk of a wet fallen tree. Next thing I knew, I was lying on the ground holding my ribs and gasping for air. I scrambled back up, but those few lost seconds would prove to be crucial.

I picked up a green coconut from the jungle floor and ran toward the men and the cars in the parking lot. It was too late. While I lay gasping for breath, the men had already set the puppies in the middle of the parking lot while the men in the cars were drift driving, doing doughnuts around the pups and blocking any chance of a possible escape. Lannie and the other two dogs were desperately trying to get to the puppies, running between cars as they passed.

Just as one of the dogs reached the pups, one of the cars steered directly toward her. I heard a loud thump and a yelp. I saw one of the females roll to a stop. She was dead.

I ran out into the middle of their makeshift raceway. No one could hear my screaming. But it didn't matter. The puppies lay flattened in the gravel.

One of the two cars came to a stop ten yards in front of me revving his engine. The other car was still joyriding, chasing the other dogs. Just as Lannie got to where one of her puppies lay dead, she was blindsided by the speeding car. She flew through the air and landed with a sickening thud. After that, she didn't move.

I stood in awe of what I had just witnessed. The world seemed to slow down around me, and my hearing faded out.

The men raised their hands in a *"What's the problem?"* gesture. The looks on their faces were cold and heartless.

I was done. I had finally been pushed over the edge. I walked toward the men.

At first they egged me on, like they were up for the challenge. I didn't care anymore. I kept walking toward them.

All of a sudden the men were scrambling to get back in their cars. The first car raced toward me like he was going to run me over. Maybe he planned to turn at the last minute to scare me. I was ready for anything. As he got near, I threw the coconut at his windshield, where it lodged halfway into the passenger compartment. The car slid to a stop and two men jumped out, ready to fight.

I already had my machete in hand. When they saw that, they jumped back in the car and raced away. The other cars took turns zooming toward me, then swerving away at the last minute. I swung the machete as the last car passed and smashed the passenger side mirror.

In the silence that followed, the dust still swirling over the gravel and the corpses of the puppies, my mind raced.

Lannie whimpered and lifted her head. She tried to get up but couldn't. I went over to her, and she tried again. She was disoriented and panting. I knelt down at her side to check the extent of her injuries. She looked past me at the puppies and whimpered through her nose. This was the first time she'd really let me hold her.

"It's okay. It's okay," I said to her over and over like a mantra. I did this whenever one of my dogs was hurt. I felt like I could transfer my calm energy to the dog this way.

Lannie had been hit in the head. Her ear and the side of her face were swollen and bleeding. She'd lost an eye.

I managed to pick her up and carry her to the edge of the jungle where she'd made her den. She lay in my lap, and I caressed her tattered body until the sun set. I had a feeling she was going to recover, but I wasn't sure how either one of us was going to live with the memory of what had just happened.

CHAPTER TWENTY

When I got home that night, I had a drink. Then I had another. It wasn't the first time, and it wouldn't be the last, that I drank to erase the nightmare of a particularly gruesome or heartbreaking experience on that beach. Between the darkness of my days with the dogs and my faulty coping mechanisms for the grief, I was changing as a person. I bit Pam's head off all the time at the tiniest provocation. And sometimes I needed a drink or three to get me through those long, hard nights of the soul.

I was determined not to become a raging alcoholic, after I'd lost my father to the bottle. But I was becoming a tough bastard to live with. I didn't envy Pam one bit.

After all, she was still trying to live her own life, survive her job, keep up with friends and coworkers, and be a loving wife, while I was becoming increasingly isolated with the dogs and my darkness and the evil that was happening at the beach. More than once, I told her she should get out while she still could. Even now, it pains me to realize that I was treating the dogs better than I treated her.

Her response to my warnings and apologies was always the same: "Don't go back to the beach. You *need* to stop going and try to get your head clear."

"I'm sorry. I can't leave the dogs."

"Steve, you have incredible street smarts, survival smarts. You can outrun pretty much anybody. But one day you're not going to pick me up from work because you chose not to outrun the wrong guy. You have to see that your anger is your Achilles' heel. You'll die in the name of the dogs."

But I didn't stop going to the beach, and somehow, thankfully, Pam found the strength to stick by me. For her, marriage was about growing old together, having a lifetime of stories to share, and staying together through the best and worst times. She understood how important saving the dogs was to me. She, in turn, was determined to save me from my own demons.

However, all I did was add stress to her life. Mondays were pizza night at the Palmas del Mar pool house with the other expats Pam worked with. I felt like an outsider and usually opted not to attend these functions. Most of the spouses (known as "trailing spouses") were women; I was one of only three men who weren't themselves employees of the company.

Whenever one of Pam's coworkers asked me how it was going with the dogs, I usually made the mistake of answering honestly. I could see by the looks on their faces that they regretted asking. But one of my fellow trailing spouses approached me during a gathering to ask about some of the stray dogs running around Palmas del Mar.

"The situation with the dogs is awful," she said. "I hate seeing them roaming around the community by themselves like that."

Finally, I thought, someone who gets it.

If only someone had interrupted our conversation right then. No dice.

She continued, "Someone needs to get rid of them, it's just not safe."

I cocked my head, not sure I understood her meaning.

"Say again?" I asked inquisitively.

"This is a really nice community, and we pay a lot of money to live here. I don't think those dogs should be allowed to roam the property, scavenging in the garbage, you know?"

"No, actually, I don't know." I was trying to keep my cool, but I didn't like where this was heading.

"All I'm saying is that they should do something about it. They should trap them or relocate them somewhere else. Just get rid of them."

The whole cool-keeping thing? Not happening.

"Maybe if more people cared enough to do something rather than bitch about them being an inconvenience or an eyesore, they wouldn't have to scavenge and beg for scraps."

She stared at me, not saying a word. Everyone within eavesdropping range stopped to listen.

"Look, I don't mean to sound like a jerk, but these animals have feelings too. I have a lot of great dogs in my care every day. They've all been to hell and back courtesy of people who didn't give a damn. I care for these dogs not because I have to, but because I want to. Some of those dogs have given their lives defending mine. So you'll have to excuse me if I've said anything to make you uncomfortable."

She stood silently, looking at me wide-eyed and blinking nervously.

"Funny thing about dogs—they'll never betray you. More than I can say about most people."

So much for our vibrant social life living in Palmas del Mar.

There were only two couples we still saw socially after that. They were sympathetic to my work with the dogs, and they were genuinely concerned for my safety and mental health. They invited us to do dinner every now and then, which helped get my mind off things and to show me firsthand that people still cared. I was disappointed in myself because of the way I'd behaved in front of Pam's colleagues. I swore to keep myself in better check.

By some miracle, I finally managed to find a veterinarian located in San Juan to look at Lannie, who had been struggling with her injuries since the day her pups were slaughtered in the boathouse parking lot. Though impatient, the vet showed some empathy after I told him what had happened. He patched up Lannie's wounded eye and took X-rays.

"She's lucky, I guess. No breaks or internal injuries, as far as I can tell," he said. "Who cleaned and sutured these wounds?"

"I did."

"Not a bad job. Did you go to vet school?"

"I'm sort of doing an internship at the beach."

I couldn't face sending Lannie back to the beach after what she'd just been through, so Pam and I took her home for a few days to heal and get her strength back.

I experienced a mixed bag of feelings having one of my dogs at the house. I felt guilty for having left all the others at the beach when they deserved a home too. But a few days later, our landlady and her son called to ask if they could come over.

"You have a dog?" she said when they came by. "You know you can't have a dog here, right? It's forbidden in your lease."

I explained what had happened to Lannie, and their expressions visibly softened.

"It's only until she get a bit better, I promise."

"Okay, but you can't keep her. A few days only."

"I know, and I really appreciate your understanding."

Then they got to the point of their visit. "We have to sell the house," she told us. "My granddaughter needs an operation on her heart. She'll die if she stays in Puerto Rico."

They needed the money from the sale of the house to send the little girl to Boston.

"We'll pay for a moving truck for you, but we have to sell fast so we can get our little one treated. I'm sorry for any inconvenience."

Two weeks later we found a new house in one of the other communities of Palmas del Mar. It felt unsettling to move again. As much as I was sick of living on the island, that first house had been a sanctuary of sorts. Now we were in another strange place with new people around us. It didn't feel like home anymore. It was also in a less well-guarded section of the compound. Anyone coming to the hotel, beach, or casino could drive right up to our front door. A tall cinder-block wall surrounded the entire property, with one side backing on the impoverished community of Candelero, which we had been warned to steer clear of. That wall was topped with coiled barbed wire. Perhaps this would reassure some people about their safety. I knew better.

One day I misplaced my keys and started to cry. It was unlike me to break down over something so trivial. "Pammie, I have to get out of here. I seriously can't stay here anymore."

"We can't just leave. I have a contract. I have an obligation to my job."

"You care more about your job than you do about me!"

"They'll fire me, Steve! Don't you get that? What will we live on?" She was furious.

At that moment I didn't care. I had to get out. I started throwing things in a big duffel bag—shorts, a winter coat, climbing gear. It made no sense. Especially since up until now, it had been Pam who'd been begging me to leave the beach.

When I looked up from the chaos I'd made of my packing, Pam was crying.

"You can't leave me!"

"But—"

"No! I will help you with the dogs, but you can't just leave me! We made a deal as a couple to be together until the end."

"I think my end is nearer than we thought it'd be." I reached for her, the craziness ebbing from my foggy brain. "And no, Pammie. I won't leave."

TWENTY-ONE

A s luck would have it, I hadn't heard the last from Martha Sampson. From time to time she e-mailed Pam, asking if we would consider starting a nonprofit organization together. With my knowledge and command of the dogs, and her making connections on the mainland from her home base in Florida, she thought we could really help the dogs of Puerto Rico. I liked the idea of doing something that would bring the plight of the *satos* into a public forum, and it would be a tremendous help if we could solicit donations toward the care and feeding of the dogs. Pam and I had been struggling for nine months to get people to take seriously what we were doing at the beach. If people here wouldn't listen or help, maybe people back home would.

However, there were long stretches of silence coming from Florida that gave us pause about the endeavor. When Martha did finally call, it was usually to ask a favor, like if we could pick up some random dog she'd heard about through a tourist who'd contacted her begging for help. I made it clear that I was unable to travel about the island looking for strays when my own workload was already more than I could handle. In her most recent call, she asked me to drive to a vet with some puppies. I didn't want any dog to suffer because of people's inability to work together, so I did what I could to accommodate her requests.

"I'd like to help, Martha, but I know that vet. He's one of the ones who made it crystal clear to me he wanted nothing to do with street dogs."

She claimed she'd worked out a deal with him, and he was willing to work with us now. I was doubtful, but I took her at her word.

"What happens to the dogs after the vet visit, Martha? Have you thought about that?"

"I think I have a place that'll take them here in Florida. Don't worry about it, I'll deal with that later."

The next day I loaded the dogs she'd asked for into crates in the back of my truck and headed off to see the vet. I arrived to find the front door locked and the lights in the office out.

I called Martha, but I kept getting her voice mail. After multiple calls, she finally answered.

"What's the deal? Do you actually have an arrangement with this guy or not? I don't have time to run fruitless errands like this, Martha."

"Please, can you just take them to your house overnight?" I could hear her crying as she spoke. "I'll sort it out, Steve. I swear."

"I can't have pets in my house, Martha. It's a violation of our lease. They have to go back to the beach." I couldn't keep the anger from my voice. "I can't have this kind of thing happen again. It's not fair to me or the dogs."

"Okay, I'm sorry. I'll call the vet in the morning and straighten this out. I promise."

When I dropped the dogs off that evening, I swore I could feel their disappointment. It was like I'd given them hope and then crushed it in one fell swoop. I could barely persuade them to get out of the truck.

I drank a lot that night. I had been through too much with these dogs, and to play with their fragile emotions was unacceptable to me.

Martha made arrangements for me to deliver the dogs to the vet the next day.

I arrived at the vet's office in Humacao a couple of hours after speaking with Martha. The vet was there this time, but he seemed irritated with me for showing up so late in the day.

"I can't do anything until tomorrow," he said. "I expected you earlier in the day. This is terribly inconvenient."

"I was asked only a couple of hours ago to bring the dogs to you for treatment. I'm just trying to help them, man. Please."

He softened his tone when he realized I was just the delivery guy. "I told Ms. Sampson this morning to get the dogs here as early as possible so I could treat them while you wait and you could take them back to the beach with you."

"What?" I was incredulous. "I was told you were going to keep the dogs at the clinic until they get a health certificate and Martha found homes for them. My instructions were only to drop them off here."

"No! No! No!" he yelled, waving his hands in the air. "I can't keep these dogs here. They are too sick. They need vaccinations." This didn't make a whole lot of sense to me considering that this was an animal hospital. "I'll need cash up front for the visit," he added.

Holy shit.

I called Martha's number from my cell multiple times, but no answer. With the vet standing there, I left increasingly angry messages on her office voice mail and her cell phone.

"Please call me back right away, Martha. It's urgent."

She didn't call.

"Can you give whatever shots the dogs need and I'll be on my way?" It was more money out of my pocket for dogs that weren't even close to ready for adoption. I had others that had been at the beach a long time who were a lot more ready for a home. Not that these dogs didn't deserve that too, but they needed more time.

An hour later, I was heading back to the beach to drop off my friends. Again.

A few days passed before Martha called me back. Even though I'd had some time to cool down, I let her have it. Through her sobs, she apologized for the misunderstanding and I let it go.

I had to admire the woman's tenacity. Soon afterward, instead of partnering with Pam and me on an organization, she actually formed one by herself and then called to ask us to do some volunteer work for her.

Hurt as I was, I put my feelings aside. This was about the dogs, not me. If she was going to help foot the bill for some of the work I was doing and get some dogs off the beach, then it was worth holding my tongue. With any luck, Martha's work would do some good in the end.

And, thankfully, it did. "Listen," she called to tell me one morning, "I've found a vet who's willing to come to the beach with a technician to neuter as many males as we can round up. All we have to do is cover her expenses and a minimal charge per dog, which I'm prepared to do."

I was amazed. She seemed to have really come through. The vet was not only willing to work with us—but to travel from clear across the island to do it.

"The only hitch is that I can't get there until the night before, so I need you to organize things on that end."

"No worries. I'm on it. Good job, Martha!"

Since Pam, Sandra, and I were the only ones in regular contact with the dogs and therefore the only ones who could handle them, we had little choice. But I welcomed this development regardless; it was a fantastic move in the right direction.

I called the vet, Sarah Paulson, myself to find out what she needed us to do. She'd only spoken briefly to Martha and didn't have a clear understanding of the logistical challenges we were facing. She had never been to my beach before, so I spent some time filling her in on the possible use of the boathouse as a makeshift hospital. On the phone, she was direct and confident and knew just what she wanted to see happen before her arrival. She was adamant about not wasting time; we would have to be as efficient and prepared as possible before she arrived.

I liked her gruff New York accent and no-bullshit style. She was the polar opposite of Martha.

"I understand completely," I assured her.

We had ten days to get things ready. The first step was taking a head count of all the males we planned to sterilize. For now we were doing only the males; the females' sterilization was a more complicated procedure and would have to wait. We'd still be cutting the new puppy population down. We were also going to give all the dogs, male and female, whatever vaccinations they needed.

Once we'd identified the males, we had to provide Sarah with a rough weight estimate of each one and an assessment of each dog's overall health.

The next phase involved preparing an operating theater. That weekend, Pam, Sandra, Sandra's husband, Angel, and I began the difficult task of cleaning the old mechanical room and some empty offices in the abandoned boathouse to use for surgery and recovery areas. It was an ambitious plan in such a short period of time. We arrived early Saturday morning with our work gloves, excited that finally this theater of cruelty was going to be turned into a place of healing.

However, the transformation was far more work than we expected. You never realize how much an object weighs until you try to move it. It turns out that equipment used to build and repair ships is bloody heavy. We used ropes and two-wheeled carts to make the job a bit easier, but by lunchtime, the heat and humidity had gotten to us. We were wrecked.

There was twenty years' worth of rusty machinery, derelict boat supplies, and broken glass all over the floor. There were rats' nests behind and under everything we moved. The boathouse had become a human toilet for beach visitors as well. It was disgusting. The whole place needed to be shoveled, swept, and disinfected. It was going to take more than the weekend to get it done. Sandra and I would need to concentrate our efforts to finish during the week.

By the following Friday, we had managed to prep and clean the rooms pretty well. I'd brought some climbing gear and suspended ropes and pulleys from the metal rafters, which we used to move the huge sheet-metal plates that had been leaning against the wall. We laid them across metal sawhorses we found in another room to fashion operating tables. I was pretty proud of what we'd been able to accomplish with a little creativity and good planning.

The last step was to beg and borrow every crate Sandra and I could get our hands on to keep the dogs contained before they were anesthetized.

A few days before our neuter clinic was to take place, Martha called.

"I don't think I can afford a hotel right now."

Pam and I thought it was strange that she hadn't planned for this ahead of time. But since she was making such a positive effort in getting this beach clinic to happen, we let it go.

"Why don't you stay with us for the weekend?" I suggested. I had a sneaking suspicion this wouldn't be the last time she'd be asking for a place to stay.

"Terrific! I'll call you when I arrive Friday night."

When she arrived, I asked, "You ready for the big day?"

"I'm a little nervous, but yeah."

I had no idea what to expect myself, but I was anxious to get started. I love the fear of the unknown.

I was the first to rise the next morning, raring to get out the door as soon as Pam and Martha were ready to leave. I knew I'd be the one coaxing the dogs into the boathouse, and there were a lot of last-minute things to be taken care of before Sarah and her vet tech arrived. Sarah had promised to bring several crates with her, but I wanted to have ours set up and waiting for her so she could start right away.

I hadn't wanted to put the dogs in the crates too early, since I was pretty sure none of them had ever been in one. So when Sarah showed up, she was annoyed that the dogs weren't crated yet.

"I've got it under control," I assured her. "When do you need the first dog?"

"Now!"

"Cool, no problem." I knew the dogs would follow me, and when I gave a whistle, they were at my side.

Sarah smiled.

"Thank you, thank you. And now for my next act . . ."

"Smart-ass," Sarah said, laughing.

I knew I was going to get along with this vet just fine.

Angel, Sandra, Pam, and I started putting the dogs in the crates while Sarah and her tech set up their space and laid out their medical supplies. Pam and Angel were standing by to help prep the dogs for surgery and assist the vet. Sandra and I were on the prowl for the dogs that had split when they saw their buddies being put in the kennels.

At one point Martha came over to me, looking frazzled.

To be fair, I had recognized a few months earlier when I first tried to help her with the dogs at the oil refinery that she wasn't exactly a natural around them. She was nervous, and they knew it. She was by her own admission a cat person, but it was obvious that she loved all animals and was doing the best she could to help. And some people just don't perform well under pressure. It was then I realized that Martha's place was behind the scenes, organizing events, raising money, but not in the trenches, where it can get pretty crazy and dirty at times. Office work may not be the spotlight position, but it's an equally important job, and I appreciated what she'd put together. It was something I hadn't been able to pull off on my own.

At the end of the day, we had sterilized more than sixty of my male dogs and vaccinated the rest of the pack. I was pretty pleased and hoped it was just the beginning.

After Sarah left, the rest of us stayed behind to look after the dogs as they awoke from anesthesia. Some took much longer than others, and it was quite a challenge to handle them as they staggered onto the beach like drunks. We couldn't let them go near the water for fear they'd drown.

I was totally beat and dehydrated from the day; I couldn't get enough fluids in me. I had a pounding headache and felt a bit emotional about what we'd managed to accomplish. I knew it would have a lasting impact on the population issues that plagued the island. But it was hard to see my dogs in pain, even though I knew it would pass soon enough. It made them vulnerable targets on this beach. I worried quietly to myself so as not to steal the joy everyone was feeling.

"You okay?" Pammie asked.

"Just trying to process everything."

It was good to see others connect with my dogs. I didn't feel so alone anymore, and I liked that.

We were all ready to crash. Martha opted to stay back with the few remaining dogs that were still waking up while the rest of us headed home. She arrived back at the house about an hour after Pam and me. While she got cleaned up, Pam and I started supper and relaxed with a glass of wine.

When Martha joined us, she too looked completely wiped out. It was clear the experience had taken an emotional toll on her as well. Considering what

I'd been through with the dogs over the previous year, I could sympathize. I hoped that this experience would help her understand what my life was like with the dogs at the beach.

The next morning, Pam and I were out the door to check on the dogs before Martha had gotten out of bed. We arrived to find most of the males hobbling around, their scrotums swollen to the size of grapefruits. On some of them, the skin had stretched to the point of splitting.

I called Sarah right away.

"It happens occasionally," she said. "The swelling will go down in time. Don't worry."

Knowing that an open wound in the tropics could lead to more serious problems in the best of times, I started all the dogs on whatever antibiotics I had on hand.

I called Martha back at the house to tell her what had happened. No answer. When Pam and I got home a while later, Martha was gone.

For several days afterward, I tried to reach Martha but to no avail. She had no way of knowing what had happened to the dogs after she'd left the island, but Pam and I were wiped out financially from the additional cost of having to buy antibiotics for more than sixty dogs. The emotional hit of losing a few of my dogs to complications pushed me back into a negative slump. I felt guilty for having done this to the dogs and angry at the lack of solutions.

"I don't want any more help with the dogs," I told Pam and Sandra afterward. No one could care for my dogs better than I did.

TWENTY-TWO

A purebred Boxer with tender traits, Evelyn was often one of the first dogs to greet me each morning on the beach. Emaciated in the beginning, she'd stagger about searching for kibble dropped or scattered by other dogs. I worked hard to put weight on her; I spoiled her with hand-feeding and special treats. I'd even massage her, manipulate her joints, and work on building her strength through gentle play and water therapy, breaking my own rules and playing favorites. I couldn't help it, I had a crush on her.

Eventually Evelyn's body began to recover. Though still horribly thin, her coat became sleek and healthy, a sign that regular meals and vitamins were beginning to have an effect.

Like the other dogs, Evelyn was hungry not just for food, but for attention. As desperate as they were for nutrients, they were always more interested in being petted than in the kibble I put in their dishes. Unlike feral dogs, these dogs had all had a taste of belonging; it explained the injured expressions on their faces and the shock and gratitude they displayed at being shown simple kindnesses. I empathized; I jumped at any kindness I felt now too.

One afternoon I had to do some errands in San Juan, so I wasn't able to spend all day with the dogs as I usually did. When I arrived back at the beach shortly before supper, I drove up the side road where I knew some of the newer and more timid dogs would stay hidden until they grew more comfortable with their surroundings. I'd usually find Evelyn here, socializing with the newbies. She had a way of welcoming them to the pack. She had the gentle nature and confidence that all pet owners wish for in their animals; the other dogs seemed to feed off her calm energy. It was clear they all loved her.

But Evelyn wasn't around. There were a few nursing mothers with their pups hiding out nearby, so I loaded up pails of food and water in the back of the truck to bring to their dens on foot. It was really strange that Evelyn wasn't there; I had seen her just that morning.

When I looked around, I could see that the other dogs didn't seem themselves. They always revealed to me when something was wrong if I just listened quietly and followed their lead.

I strolled through the boathouse toward the deserted shipyard on the other side. Some of the dogs seemed to hesitate near the entrance to the old mechanical room. A few of them walked into the room that we had cleaned last month for the neuter clinic. They sniffed the air and whimpered. I backtracked to investigate.

As I rounded the corner, I saw Evelyn lying on the cold concrete floor. The world around me went silent. My heart and thoughts began to race. I startled myself when I heard myself say, "No. Oh, sweetie. No."

I walked over and knelt at her side. She was dead. I would have to call Pam and tell her I'd be late so I could bury my poor, sweet girl.

And then I did a double take. There was a bed sheet pulled up over her lower body, and she was lying on a fresh beach towel. I wiped away my tears and saw the gentle rise and fall of her chest. *She's alive!* She was unconscious, but she was breathing.

I carefully lifted the sheet. It appeared a car had crushed her hindquarters. I figured her head had to have taken a blow too, enough to knock her out.

I called Sandra to see if she knew what had happened.

"I found her by the side of the road near the entrance to the parking lot."

"When was this? I was here this morning."

"I was running late today. Must have been around lunchtime, I guess."

It must have happened right after I left for San Juan.

"I didn't know what else to do. I called Sonia to help me carry her to the boathouse. I didn't want to leave her out in the open."

I took a moment to collect myself. I was angry, but not at Sandra: it was this hellhole the dogs had to live in and the people who found pleasure in hurting them that fueled my rage. I knew Sandra would never do anything to harm the dogs. We were both doing everything in our power to help them and faced hard decisions on the beach every day. I knew Sandra didn't have any money for a vet. Not that it even mattered. What kind of life was Evelyn going to have, even if she recovered? Who would take her?

I sat with Evelyn well into the night, my hand resting on her rib cage. It was dark, the only light coming from a patch of moonlight shining through the doorless opening, but I felt safe with my pack at my side. I knew they could feel my pain and the pain of their fallen friend. At that moment life seemed very unfair. These dogs had done nothing to deserve this tortured life. There are shitty people all over the world who have it good, but these dogs? It didn't seem right.

I hoped that Evelyn would peacefully pass away in the night while she was still unconscious. I didn't want her to suffer. I also didn't want to be the guy who had to make the decision to end her life. I often felt that finding these dogs on the beach was like Achates' legacy, that he lived on through the work we did helping other dogs. When times were tough at the beach, I'd find myself asking him for strength.

I needed to go home to Pam. I had stayed at the beach much later than I ever had in the eleven months I'd been on the island. I felt terrible leaving Evelyn alone on the floor, but I had no choice. There was nothing I could do for her. The dogs stretched and yawned and walked me back to the truck.

At home, I peeled off my clothes and took a shower. I let the cool water run over my body. I was tired. Not a normal tired, but the bone-crushing kind of tired that comes with depression. I needed something to take the edge off, to numb me a bit.

Pam brought me a glass of scotch and I talked. She didn't say anything; she just looked very sad for me. She could feel my pain too.

"Why is this bothering me so much? I mean, I get it, I love Evelyn. But I've buried so many dogs. What's so different this time?"

And then it hit me: When I'd buried those other dogs, they had already been dead when I found them. Evelyn was still alive, still suffering, and I was doing nothing to help her. Initially I'd been upset at Sandra for leaving her alone, and now I'd done the same thing. I lay awake all night thinking about what to do.

First thing in the morning, I dropped Pam at a coworker's house to get a ride to work. I had to get to the beach.

The dogs greeted me as usual. I quickly and somewhat carelessly laid their food out for them, then made my way to where I'd left Evelyn the night before.

She was still breathing. Shallowly, but breathing. She was such a good girl, such a fighter to have survived nearly starving to death and whatever abuse she'd experienced living on the street. Now this.

I walked to an area of the beach that had cell reception and called Martha. After all the favors I'd done for her, it was time to call in a chit. When, as usual, my calls went to her voice mail, I tried calling a couple of vets myself, but I could never get past the receptionist.

I tried Martha again later. At last, she answered.

"Sandra told me what happened," she said when I told her about Evelyn.

"Can you talk to your vet? He's not taking my calls, and we can't just leave her here. She needs to be euthanized, Martha." I wanted the vet to come to the beach, to do it before she woke up and felt the pain of her injuries.

"Sandra thinks she'll be all right when she wakes up. We should give her a fighting chance."

I wish I could say I respected that line of thinking, but I couldn't. It was selfish.

"Martha, she was crushed. The most humane thing we can do is end her suffering."

"Let's wait and see how she does, Stephen. We can make a decision when she wakes up. I know an organization that helped a dog with similar injuries—they got a wheelchair apparatus so he could walk."

Did she just start talking about wheelchairs?

"Evelyn is a street dog, Martha. People didn't want to help her *before* she was run over by a car. What makes you think anyone will go to such extremes for her now?"

Martha started crying. "The only reason I didn't do anything before is that I had no money."

I went off. "So how much money do you have *now*? Do you think vet bills, rehab, and doggy wheelchairs are all going to be free?"

All I heard was sobbing on the other end of the line.

"Martha, I know these dogs better than anyone. I owe it to Evelyn to give her the dignity she deserves. Please! I'm begging you to call the vet and ask him to come down here."

"Let's wait until I hear back about the wheelchair."

My final words to her weren't pretty. I hung up.

I went back to Evelyn. Nothing had changed. I talked quietly to her, petted her face, and begged her to let go.

I arrived home late and in need of a drink, as I had the night before.

When I got back to the boathouse in the morning, Evelyn raised her head from the floor. I was surprised and happy to see her smiling face, but I could immediately sense her distress and pain. The look in her eyes was a plea for help. I lay on the filthy floor next to her and held her head. I couldn't help but feel I had failed her.

I was desperate, so I called Martha again.

"I'm still waiting to hear about the wheelchair," she chirped.

I held my tongue. I begged her to call the vet.

A couple of hours later, she called back. "Can you take Evelyn to the vet's office? I've made arrangements to pay for the visit."

I was alone, and Evelyn was a big dog. I knew that any movement would be agony. I wasn't willing to do that to her.

"Is there any way you can convince him to come here? I can't move her."

A short while later, she called back. "Okay, he's coming. Can you meet him on the side of the freeway by the toll booth near Palmas del Mar and show him the way?"

I waited nearly two hours, but at last he arrived, and he followed me to the beach. Once again, Evelyn was clearly happy to see me. The vet had a quick look at her.

"You made the right decision." The injuries were too extensive. Her spine and pelvis were crushed, and her internal organs were shutting down. I could have guessed all this, but now I felt a little better about choosing to end her life.

As the vet injected the lethal dose into a vein in her front leg, I held Evelyn's face, stared into her eyes, and told her how much I loved her. Within moments, I felt her spirit leave her body. I spoke softly, "No more pain, sweetie."

The vet got up and walked back to his truck without a word. I was alone, holding Evelyn.

I carried her to the graveyard and buried her, my dogs at my side the entire time. They were very quiet. I sat in the sand with the pack until dark. I was exhausted.

In the days that followed, I ran into Sandra and Sonia at the beach. They were sad about Evelyn, and questioned what I'd done.

"I wish you had given God a chance to heal her," Sonia said, with Sandra translating for me. (Since I spent 90 percent of my waking hours with the dogs, I never mastered Spanish the way I'd intended when we got to Puerto Rico.)

I didn't want to argue with her. She believed what she believed. I knew it wasn't the last time I'd have a conversation like this. The choice to humanely euthanize a dog is controversial in the rescue world. I hadn't experienced it until now. But I never doubted that I'd done the right thing by Evelyn, just as I'd done the right thing by my beloved Achates in the end.

TWENTY-THREE

Around this time, I got an e-mail from a woman named Melanie Shapiro in San Juan. Months earlier, Betsy Freedman, the Save a Sato representative in Boston, had promised me, "Help is on the way." As it turned out, Melanie was that help.

Melanie worked with a group that rescued stray cats in Old San Juan. But she also had contacts at a privately run rescue shelter near San Juan, and she wanted to take some of my dogs there. However, as I learned in our initial exchange, Melanie lived over an hour away and didn't have a car, so I wasn't sure exactly how she was going to be able to help me at my beach. And given my experience with Martha, I was doubly wary of another outsider's intentions, however good they might be.

But as always, the dogs came first, and I couldn't turn Melanie away without giving her a chance. When I spoke with her on the phone a few days later, we made a plan for her to come and see my dogs for herself.

One morning at the end of the week, I drove to San Jan to pick her up. She'd given me an address, and told me to wait in the car for her. I arrived on time, and waited. And waited. I didn't really want to bug her, but after forty-five minutes cooling my heels in the truck, I relented and called her cell. No answer.

Then, a few moments after I hung up, she appeared on the balcony of her apartment.

"I'll be right down! I'm just getting a cup of tea!"

Judging from her obvious bed head, I figured she hadn't even gotten up yet, at least not until I'd called and woken her up. It wasn't her fault that I hate when people make me wait, but I'd gotten up extra early and driven ninety minutes through brutal rush hour traffic to get here, and, to make matters worse, I was now really late to feed the dogs. I had a set schedule with them, and I knew they counted on it. I didn't appreciate wasting my time waiting for a stranger.

Finally, Melanie came down. As she approached the car, I took note that she was wearing shorts and flip-flops, exactly what I had suggested she *not* wear to the beach. Caring for the dogs was tough, dirty work. And her fair, freckled skin was going to take a beating in the tropical midday sun. But I wasn't her father, so I didn't say anything. She lived on the island, so I figured she knew what she was doing.

"I hope you don't mind, I asked Mary Eldergill to meet us. She's another rescuer from the south side of the island," she said on the drive to Yabucoa.

Great, that's all I needed, another do-gooder getting in the way of what really needed to be done. I guess my skepticism showed on my face.

"Don't worry, she's a veteran at this. She's been rescuing dogs for more than twenty years."

As I navigated the long narrow approach road to the beach, I rolled the window down and whistled for my pack. They popped out of the vegetation and fell in line along the side and rear of the truck as I pulled into the parking area near the metal storage containers. I jumped out and got my usual hero's welcome.

Melanie stayed in the truck, her mouth agape. I couldn't tell if she was impressed or apprehensive. It was *a lot of dogs*.

"You can get out," I said. "The dogs are fine."

She didn't budge, so I went around to the passenger side and opened the door for her.

"Are they contagious?" she asked as she stepped gingerly from the vehicle. I was surprised by her unease given her experience rescuing street dogs.

"I told you to wear long pants and real shoes."

"Oh my God. I had no idea there'd be so many dogs. They look awful. What happened to them?"

Clearly she'd forgotten, or ignored, our phone conversation.

"I did warn you," I said.

"Well, you know, Steve, sometimes people exaggerate."

"I knew it! I had a feeling you didn't really believe me when we talked on the phone."

This is where the situation got weird. My powers of observation had gotten pretty good over the last year, and if there was one thing I could spot at a distance, it was a non–dog person. Melanie's body language was defensive and her tone of voice was strained. She held her hands in tight fists under her chin as she repeated, "There's a good doggie, there's a good doggie," over and over. What the hell was she even doing here?

Her vibe was transferring to the dogs, and some of the more hyper ones were getting a little frenzied, which was annoying the alphas—exactly how fights started.

"Melanie? You're not going to make me regret bringing you here, are you?" I said it calmly with a half smile, but I wanted it to be obvious to her that I was serious. "Just shadow me, get to know the dogs by watching them, okay? No talking, no touching, no eye contact with the dogs. You relax and they'll relax. It's easy." I fully trusted my dogs to behave well toward her, but I didn't want them fighting because she'd gotten them into a funky mood.

A few hours passed, and still no sign of Melanie's friend Mary. Meanwhile, Melanie's lack of preparation for the day was manifesting itself all over the place. First there was the bad clothing and shoes. But she'd also forgotten to bring the snacks, water, and sunblock I'd told her to on the phone. I had to give her some lotion I had in the truck, and, as the day wore on, she worked her way through my own water and snack provisions.

I was pretty close to fed up and about to suggest we pack it in when, lo and behold, a beat-up old VW van came zooming into the lot. The driver's-side' door opened to reveal Mary, her wild, frizzy hair blowing in the sea breeze and a crazy-ass crooked smile. Even though she was hours and hours late, it was impossible to stay mad at this woman.

I immediately led her on a tour of the beach.

"I've been doing this a long, long time, Steve, and this is by far the worst I've ever seen."

"I know some of them look pretty bad, but they're in a lot better shape now than they were when I first found them."

It was then that Mary noticed my beautiful white shepherd, Jess. When Pam and I had found him months earlier, he was afraid of his own shadow and couldn't be touched. We guessed that someone had thrown boiling oil over his back and neck, and he was covered in horrible third-degree burns. Once, I'd been standing in line at a food vendor when a street dog had gotten too close to the food stand. The vendor's wife got angry and threw a ladle of hot oil at the dog. Fortunately, the dog was fast that day and got out of the way in time. I had a feeling Jess hadn't been so lucky.

As if the burns weren't enough, Jess had several gashes across his flanks, likely the result of a machete. Since knife wounds were pretty common among my dogs, I had made it a point to learn how to suture. I'd been buying pig parts at the grocery store and practicing my stitching skills on them. I'd gotten damn good at it.

The day I met Jess, I'd gone home to do some Internet research on treating severe burns. It took a while for Jess to trust me, but once he did, I was able to treat and suture his flank wounds. Then came the difficult task of scrubbing the wounds clean and dressing his burns with antibiotic cream every single day. Most of the time he would howl in agony and try to get away, and when I was done the little bugger would promptly roll in the sand, but over time it was apparent that he was slowly healing. The remarkable thing was that no matter how much he protested the treatment, or how much pain he must have been in, he never once growled at me or bit me, not even when I had to trim the edges of his flesh and scrape his wounds to suture them properly shut.

Poor Jess was still covered in ugly battle scars.

"I can't believe what a sweetheart he is," Mary said when I told her Jess's story. "After what he's been through? Amazing." I was really happy that my dogs liked her, which I always took as a good sign.

Mary opened the side door of her van and started pulling out plastic tubs filled with medical supplies, which we spent the rest of the day using on the dogs. We gave them vaccinations, vitamin boosters, and dewormer. In no time I was overloaded with information and supplies I could only have dreamed of in the past. Evidently Mary had some connection that supplied her with dog medications.

"You are most definitely the Mother Teresa of dogs," I said.

It was getting late, and we'd done more than I ever thought possible. I was exhausted but beaming like a kid in a candy store. It had been a long time since I'd felt so hopeful.

"Okay, let's figure out who I can take with me today," Mary said, scanning the pack.

"What?" I was a little taken aback.

"You can't take care of this many dogs by yourself, Steve. I have a few spaces at my place."

She chose the motherless puppies and a few of the smaller dogs. I had no idea how many dogs this lady had managed to save in all the years she'd been rescuing. All I knew was that she was helping more in this one trip than anyone had done in the entire previous year.

"Mary, what do I owe you for the medication?"

"Nothing, Steve. I've got this."

I was overwhelmed with gratitude as I helped her load the dogs into her van.

She got in and started to pull away, then stopped and stuck her head out the window.

"Hey, Steve! Why don't you and your wife break away from here after your morning rounds Saturday and come see me in Salinas. I've got more meds I'd like to give you for your dogs. I really didn't know what to expect today, so I didn't bring everything with me. And you can meet *my* pack."

When she drove off, I was left standing with Melanie, surrounded by dogs. It was now up to me to decide which ones were about to get a get-out-of-jail-free pass and go with Melanie for eventual homes back in the States. It was impossibly difficult choosing which dogs to take. I loved them all.

In the end, we loaded the remaining motherless pups into my truck for the drive back to San Juan. As I drove away, the dogs left behind gave me a look that was more heart wrenching than usual, so I was quiet during the ride. I wanted to be excited about the day's accomplishments, but I found it difficult to muster up the energy to pull it off. Melanie's optimistic attitude had vanished several hours earlier, when she'd realized that the dog problem at the beach was much bigger than she'd expected. She was tense and cranky with the dogs barking in the back of the truck. We arrived at the shelter a little over an hour later, unloaded our precious cargo, then continued on into San Juan to drop Melanie back at her place.

On the ride home, my heart ached. As wonderful as it was that so many dogs had got a new lease on life today, with the promise of a real home down the road, there were so many left to their own devices on that dangerous beach. I knew that many of them would die before the next rescue mission arrived. I would never utter my misgivings out loud for fear of sounding un-grateful—I was more than grateful for what these gals had done for me and my dogs—but as usual, it was complicated.

TWENTY-FOUR

A year into our Puerto Rico sojourn, taking care of the dogs was my full-time job; I did little to nothing else. The dogs depended on me, and I had come to depend on them too. There was something very healing for me about being with them. Until now I had never been able to re-create the feeling of purpose I'd had when working with orphaned kids in Southeast Asia years earlier. Instead of thinking only of myself, my days had been scheduled around taking care of children who had nothing. Now I felt alive again, like I was doing something that could make a difference in the world, that my actions actually mattered. Even if only to the dogs and me, I was making a difference.

As difficult as it was for me emotionally to bury the dogs, it was a job that needed to be done on a daily basis. The week following Mary and Melanie's visit was no exception. Some of the dogs that were too far gone when I met them passed away during the night. Some of the dogs I had nurtured back to health had been killed deliberately; some of them had received loving pats from Mary and been promised they would be on the next shipment off this miserable beach. I felt like I had betrayed them.

Often, when I was carrying a dog to the hole I'd dug, my mind would flash back to when I was a child and felt the need to run like hell from my fears. I had never actually been afraid of dying myself; it was more the fear of losing someone I loved. My dad. My grandpa. My childhood pets. I didn't want to be left alone without them. Every time, I had run until I fell from exhaustion. I'd lie there until dark and then walk home, often not getting back to my house until the wee hours of the morning. My family had worried about me, but they knew that if they chased me I'd go even farther and stay away longer. I could only imagine how hard it must have been for Mum and Nan to keep it together and be strong for us boys after Dad and Grandpa died. I remember hearing them cry alone behind closed doors when they thought we couldn't hear. But somehow they put on a brave face and remained strong for us kids and got us through incredibly tough times. I had always wished I could summon the kind of strength they had displayed.

Now I was being forced to face this fear of loss and confront my demons head-on. The dogs had no one else to take care of them when they died. I was beginning to identify different feelings I had each time I carried a dog to its grave, or held one in my arms as it died. It had begun when Pam and I had to put Achates to sleep. I had lain on the vet's office floor, holding his face and looking into his eyes. I didn't want him to go, but I knew in my heart it was time. The urge to run was almost too much to resist. But I needed to be there for him, and for Pam. I lay there with Achates for over an hour after he fell into his forever sleep. He lay there with such calm confidence and peace, I felt his energy flow through me and calm me enough to stay at his side. I never forgot that feeling, and relied on it now.

My daughter Bethany (from a previous marriage) and her boyfriend Ryan wanted to come visit for my birthday. I hadn't met Ryan yet, and I hadn't seen Bethany in a long time, so I was really looking forward to it. Neither of them had traveled far outside their small hometown in the American Northwest, let alone out of the country. I thought this would be a great opportunity for them to experience our island life and broaden their horizons.

I've always loved to people watch, and the San Juan airport is a great place to do that. Whether it was a gaggle of tourists being shepherded to the sheltered quarters of a cruise ship or a seasoned business traveler striding confidently to the car rental desk, it was fun to guess each person's comfort—or discomfort—level. Pam and I would sometimes make up scenarios for the people we saw, role-playing conversations we imagined they were having.

Bethany and Ryan were pretty entertaining to watch, like two deer in the headlights, as you might imagine a young couple traveling out of the country for the first time would be. They looked quite relieved to see me on the other side of the glass in the baggage claim area. And I was happy to see them and excited about all I had planned for their visit. First up, the joyride that was the trip to Yabucoa.

As we got into my truck, I said, "Ladies and gentlemen, at this time I'd like to ask you to stow your bags, put your seats and tray tables in the upright position, and please fasten your seat belts securely as we are ready for takeoff."

The kids chuckled at my stupid Dad humor, not giving it much thought until we exited the parking garage.

The drive to Palmas del Mar was nothing out of the ordinary for me, but for them it was like a real-life amusement park ride. Bethany white-knuckled the dashboard, and Ryan did the same on the back of the seat.

"Enjoying the ride?" I said. I guess I could have warned them what driving was like in Puerto Rico, but I figured why spoil the surprise?

"How does anyone get where they're going without an accident here?" Bethany said, her voice a little tremulous with fear.

"Don't jinx it! We're not home yet!" I said smiling.

We arrived in one piece. When we drove through the entrance gates to the compound, the kids' fear turned to awe.

"Oh my God, you live here?"

I laughed. "Don't be too impressed. Consider it more of a white-collar prison with benefits."

It was kind of fun to see how excited they were about where they'd be staying on their vacation.

Over the next few days, Bethany and Ryan joined me on my morning rounds with the dogs, and then we headed off to explore the island. I could tell they were trying to embrace every new experience I threw their way, and I was determined to help them change their small-town view of the world and their preconceived notions about other ethnicities and cultures. I avoided the typical touristy things people usually do when they come to the island on vacation, instead taking them kite surfing and snorkeling at out-of-the-way spots. Wherever we went during their stay, I made stops at some of my favorite street vendors for lunch. The roadside food stands sold amazing homemade dishes, often displayed in the kind of aquariums people generally keep pet fish in. Usually the vendors had a wood-burning grill right there. What was most fun for me was the places where I was considered a regular: the vendors didn't speak English, and I still had no Spanish under my belt, and yet we communicated beautifully and I was treated like family.

I was heartened to see how open-minded Bethany and Ryan were. I only wished I'd been able to give my kids more of this type of experience when they were little, but, as a divorced dad, I only had them with me for six weeks in the summer and every other Christmas.

In 1986, at the end of my three years with the orphans in Southeast Asia, I had returned home to Canada to recover from the malaria I'd contracted. Not long after that, I got a girl I barely knew pregnant. Determined to do right by her, I married her. It was a bad idea. In no time we had a second child. By the time I was twenty-four, we were divorced, and my kids grew up traveling between two families and sharing holidays. So I welcomed the chance to have an adult relationship with my now grown-up daughter, and to share my world with her.

In the middle of Bethany's visit, I got a call from Melanie saying that she wanted to bring her friend Monica from the World Society for the Protection of Animals to the beach. Apparently the WSPA representative had heard about the crazy gringo with a hundred dogs, and she was going to come to the island specifically to meet me. I welcomed the visit and promised to make time to show her around.

On the appointed morning, I brought the kids with me to the beach to get the dogs fed and settled before Melanie and her guest arrived.

Just as we were filling the buckets with food and water, an unfamiliar car rolled up right behind us. Always anxious about strangers who were up to no good, my hackles tingled when I couldn't see inside the passenger compartment past the glare of the windshield.

And then Melanie stepped out, laughing. "You didn't know it was us, did you?"

A pretty Hispanic woman stepped out of the driver's side. "Hi. I'm Sylvia. You must be Steve."

We shook hands. "Welcome," I said, the nerves of a few seconds earlier quickly dissipating into relief.

"I've heard a lot of good things about you and your dogs."

"I'm about halfway through morning rounds. You're welcome to tag along while I finish up, though."

"It's amazing how much control you have over so many dogs, Steve," Sylvia said after a few minutes of observing my routine. I had nearly eighty dogs in the pack at this point. I gave her the backstories on each animal in turn. Like Mary before her, Sylvia was drawn particularly to Jess, the beautiful white shepherd who'd been so badly burned. Sylvia too was appalled by what I told her.

While we were talking, another car drove up, several men hanging out the windows, throwing bottles and shouting at the dogs standing on the side of the road. The car swerved for the dogs and just missed. Not satisfied, they made a U-turn and went for the dogs a second time. I tore through the parking lot on foot to cut these guys off. To my surprise, Sylvia was right there next to me, shouting at the men in Spanish. They pulled to a stop, exchanged a few heated words with her, then drove away.

"What did you say to them?" I asked.

"I told them we had their plate number and had called the police."

I was impressed.

"You can hang out here any time you like," I said. Sylvia stayed with the dogs and me for the rest of the day. She was a natural on the beach: passionate, tough, and lacking the patronizing attitude toward the animals that drove me crazy.

"Please come back anytime," I said at the end of the day, giving her a hug.

"I will. And I'll try to get you some help down here, okay?"

TWENTY-FIVE

M y time with Bethany and her boyfriend came to an end, and I resumed my normal routine. It wasn't long before Melanie called again requesting I give yet another "Steve tour" of the beach for someone named Nancy Guilford, whom she'd met at an animal rights function in San Juan. Melanie had told her about my dogs, particularly Nina and Nicole, and Nancy wanted to help.

"She could be a big help, Steve. She's got money," Melanie said.

"Okay, but please don't keep me waiting again. Be here at nine A.M." I didn't mean to sound ungrateful—I was always willing to do whatever it took to get the dogs some much-needed help—but each day I had a laundry list of tasks to accomplish, and a glitch in the schedule could throw the whole day off.

Melanie chuckled. "I'll do my best. But no promises."

This didn't bode well.

I got to the beach around 7:30 A.M. to prep the dogs and get them settled for the day. I wasn't taking as much time with them as I normally did, so I could be ready for our visitors. Shortly before nine, I drove back up the road to where I'd made the den for Nina and Nicole and waited. The girls were still pretty sick and grew tired quickly after breakfast. After an hour waiting by the side of the road, the dogs wandered back to their den to sleep.

Moments later, Melanie and Nancy pulled up in a Ford Explorer. I was pissed off, and I'm sure it showed on my face.

"I know! I know! I'm late. There, we got that out of the way."

I kept scowling.

"Steve, this is Nancy. Nancy, this is Steve."

Nancy handed me a business card for her rescue group. She was pretty, perfectly coiffed, and overdressed in a pair of designer jeans tucked into a pair of really expensive-looking red leather designer boots. She didn't look like any rescuer I'd ever met. I would later learn that Nancy was a schoolteacher who had moved to the island a few years earlier. Her plans had changed when she met and married a wealthy land developer who'd been living on the island for about ten years. She initially started volunteering with Save a Sato, but found the organization too dysfunctional, so she started her own. Basically, she grabbed strays off the street and took them to an expensive vet in San Juan, paying whatever it took to get the dogs healthy. Her heart was definitely in the right place. But, like me, she had no long-term plan in place.

Given the delay, I skipped the preliminaries and jumped right in. "I want you to meet a couple of my worst-case dogs. Don't be alarmed by their appearance. They look pretty rough, but they're good girls."

"I'm fine. I've seen it all before."

I gave a whistle and within seconds Nina and Nicole were poking their heads out of the dense jungle foliage. They came trotting up to us, tails wagging.

Melanie didn't show any emotion, but Nancy started to weep as she knelt down to cuddle the dogs. I was glad she wasn't put off by their appearance; some folks were afraid to touch them, thinking their skin conditions were contagious. But Nancy pulled them close to her face and talked to them as if they were babies, which had the unfortunate effect of riling the dogs up. Nina and Nicole started to pull away from her grasp, looking to me for guidance.

"Hey, Nancy, I know you're really feeling the dogs' pain, but you need to do your best to be strong for them, okay? Your energy is all wrong, and you're starting to upset them."

She got up off her knees. "I was just trying to get to know them."

"I understand, but they need us to be calm. Getting them worked up just drains their energy unnecessarily."

Nina and Nicole were by my side now, awaiting my next move.

"You'll notice I say very little to them. They read my body language and my energy without the clutter of a lot of words. See how calm they are now?"

I couldn't blame her for being a little put off by my lecturing, but it needed to be said. In any event, she was undeterred, and I admired her for that.

"I'd like to take them to Dr. Ramos, my vet in San Juan," Nancy said.

"Really? That's awesome. There's nothing I want more than to see these girls get the proper care they deserve. What will you do with them after their stay at the vet?"

"I don't know yet," Nancy said.

Melanie piped up, "Betsy gave me the names of some shelters in New York, New Jersey, and Florida that might be interested in working with street dogs from here. I'll reach out to them."

"Perfect!" I said. "I've been trying to do that for months, but they don't seem to have any interest in helping independent rescuers like me."

Nancy had brought a few large travel crates along just in case there were dogs she could take back with her. I opened the back of her truck and unloaded the two biggest. I set them on the ground and began unfastening the nuts holding the top half to the bottom.

"Hey, Steve!" Melanie barked. "What are you doing? We just put those together!"

"These dogs have been through hell and back several times already. I don't think they're going to be too happy jumping into the crates without an introduction."

"Steve, we don't have much time, and you're wasting it now. Can't you just put them in?"

"Maybe if you'd been on time, Melanie, this wouldn't be a problem."

"Big deal, we got a late start. Get over it already."

"It is a big deal, Melanie, if it affects how the dogs are treated."

"I'm sorry, it's my fault," Nancy chimed in. "I made us stop at Starbucks, and we lost track of time."

It wasn't much of a reason, but I appreciated Nancy's attempt to defuse the situation. The fact was, I desperately needed the help she was offering, so I needed to focus on that.

"It's important that the dogs are properly introduced to being in a crate for the first time. They need to know they that can go in and out freely without feeling constricted," I explained a little more calmly. "It'll give them a comfort level they wouldn't have if we just crammed them in there."

I lay the bottom half of the kennel on the ground and gently encouraged the girls to go in and out as they pleased. Within a few moments they were comfortably curled up in a ball awaiting the top and door to be installed on their temporary dens.

"Now that's how it's done! You're hired!" Nancy said with a big smile.

In the end, it took only a few extra minutes to introduce the girls to the crates. Once they were secured in the back of Nancy's truck, we headed to the beach, Nancy following me in her vehicle. She wanted to meet the rest of the dogs and see if there were others she could take back to San Juan with her.

She'd barely come to a stop before she was out the door and running toward the pack, doing the baby talk thing again. Some of the dogs started barking at her to keep away.

"Nancy, stop! Just wait a second, okay?"

I calmed the dogs down.

"Are you ready to meet them properly now?" I asked her. "I'm not trying to be obnoxious about this, I swear. It's part of the training, so that someday they'll be ready to be house pets." I never let the dogs jump on me or anyone else.

I had always hoped that I would be able to provide more than just food, water, and medical care for the dogs, so whatever I thought about the appropriateness of Nancy's approach to the dogs, the important thing was that she was going to get some of them off this horrible beach. She chose a few of the younger, healthier dogs to take with her. I wasn't going to argue with any of her choices. I mean, hell, she had Nina and Nicole enjoying the nice air-conditioning in the back of her truck already. I would be forever grateful to

Nancy for taking on the two hardest cases of abuse and neglect I'd ever seen. Nina and Nicole had come a long way in the seven months since I'd found them in the middle of the road, emaciated, dehydrated, mangy to the point of hairlessness, and totally disoriented. So many times I'd dreaded the thought of arriving at the beach to find them dead. I loved those two girls as much as any dog I'd ever had.

As Nancy was getting ready to leave, I opened the back of the truck to say good-bye to the girls and wish them luck on their journey to their new lives and forever homes. I could barely swallow; the lump in my throat from trying to hold back tears was actually painful. I had to be strong for them a bit longer. I could feel the girls' thanking me for saving them as I looked in their eyes and cuddled their faces one last time. They each gave my cheek a lick.

"We've gotta get rolling if we're going to get back before Dr. Ramos's office closes," Nancy said.

I closed the back door of Nancy's SUV.

"Hey, Nancy, one last thing," I said.

"Yes? What's that?"

"You have to make sure they stay together, okay? At least while they're at the vet's recovering. I think they survived because of each other."

"I promise. And I'll do everything I can to find a family that'll take them both."

I gave both Nancy and Melanie a hug. "I'm sorry I was so sharp with you earlier," I said, and walked with my pack to the metal storage containers, out of the way. I finally allowed the tears to fall when she drove down the beach road and out of sight. In the end, I was tremendously grateful to Nancy for taking the girls to the vet and footing the bill. That was enough to make me forget the trip to Starbucks.

Caring for the dogs over this past year, I had experienced more than my share of emotional and physical breakdowns. Increasingly, I had overreacted to situations that I would normally have overlooked, barking at Pam, getting her in trouble at work, getting into potentially violent confrontations with random strangers who crossed me. I could feel the change in my heart, but I felt my ability to control it slipping out of reach. I found myself pushing boundaries more and more lately. It was scaring everyone who knew and loved me—my brothers, my mum, and Pam most of all. If Pam hadn't been so committed to our marriage, to supporting me no matter what, she might well have kicked me out, and I wouldn't have blamed her.

With every day that passed, I was faced with more death, more burials, and more newcomers to the pack. It cut deep into my heart that I had to leave them each day. The dogs would follow alongside and behind the truck as I drove away. As soon as they were safely out of harm's way, I would gun the engine as fast as I could so they wouldn't keep following. I knew they were safer at the beach than on the road, where drivers would deliberately swerve to hit them. I didn't want them to waste their precious energy chasing me either. More than once I'd had to turn back to collect a few of the dogs that had chased the truck too far up the road.

Sometimes my mind played games with me. Was I any better than those heartless people who abandoned the dogs in the first place? I felt like every day I got their hopes up, only to crush them again when I drove away. At least today, some of those dogs had had their futures handed back to them.

Nancy and Melanie made a couple of additional trips to the beach later that month. Between their efforts and Mary's we got a total of thirty-two dogs off the beach, seen by a vet, and relocated, either temporarily to privately run shelters on the island, or to stateside shelters. But it wasn't easy going.

I appreciated the help I was getting, and I knew my job was to continue preparing the dogs for their new homes. During those weeks, I had to make some hard choices. Nancy and Melanie were always drawn to the smaller, cuter dogs, regardless of how long they'd been at the beach or whether they were ready to go or not. The women had a tendency to rush in and out. I tried to understand that they didn't want to spend any more time than necessary in this depressing place, but they didn't know the dogs like I did. At first I held my tongue, but on the third trip, when they were loading several of the newest dogs into the crates, I finally asked if they'd discuss their choices with me.

"I'm concerned because I've only just met these dogs and I know they have a few issues I need address before they go. I haven't had a chance to work one-on-one with them yet."

"So?" Melanie said.

"Have you seen this one eat?" I said, pointing to one of the little dogs. "He's got pretty serious food aggression issues. He'll go after you if you approach him when there's food around. A few of them are like that when they first get here."

"No way, he's too sweet," Nancy said. "Look at this little baby boy."

She had set a sausage treat on top of the crate as she opened the door. Apparently, she was going to prove me wrong. The dog was wriggling around in his crate, responding to her baby talk, as dogs will when they feel anxious. She reached in, pulled him out, and began nuzzling his face.

"See? How can you say that about this sweetie little muffin?"

She was looking at me, not the dog, when she reached for the treat. He saw what she had in her hand, and his body immediately stiffened, his eyes fixated on the food.

"Nancy! I seriously advise against giving him that treat. Especially while you're holding him. It'll end badly. Put the dog down!"

She shook her head and made a sarcastic face at me. As she brought the snack nearer the dog's reach, he went berserk. It reminded me of the way a shark will attack a seal in the open ocean. It's a very deliberate and violent act, done without much warning.

Nancy screamed and dropped the dog, who dropped the treat in midair. As soon as he hit the ground, he stood guard over it, baring his teeth and growling like a wild dog. He gobbled the treat down with ferocity, and then trotted happily back to Nancy for more loving.

Nancy was shaking like a leaf, a stunned look on her face.

"Are you all right?" I asked, but I felt worse for the dog than I did for her. It could have been a lot worse. She was lucky she wasn't bitten in the face.

As usual, Nancy and Melanie didn't seem to take me very seriously. To them, I was just the guy who fed the dogs.

"Come here. Let me show you something." I was reaching for a bag of treats that had slipped down the side of the crate in the back of the truck. I gave a whistle and my pack leaders were at my side right away. "Watch!" I snapped my fingers and made a sweeping hand gesture to the pack. The dogs' rear ends hit the ground so fast I bet most designer-dog owners would have been jealous. I knelt down in front of Leo, put one of the treats between my lips, and parked my face inches from his nose. He waited patiently for my okay before he gently nuzzled the treat from me. The only evidence that he'd been there was a trace of slobber on my lips.

"Did you see that?" I heard Melanie whisper to Nancy. "How cool was that?"

I did this little food trick with more than a dozen of the larger, previously overlooked dogs. They were the ones Melanie and Nancy had declined to take during their previous rescue trips. I had spent a year with these dogs, patiently training them so that if the opportunity ever arrived, they'd be ready to be adopted someday. Until that moment, Melanie and Nancy had had no idea what I really did with the dogs all day at the beach. From then on, they asked my opinion about which dogs were ready to go.

I felt bad that the four dogs they had selected to take that day weren't ready to go. I had to pull them out of the truck and put them back with the pack. They hadn't done anything wrong; they just weren't ready to be handled yet. I knew how strict most stateside shelters are about dogs with food aggression; if we were to send these dogs on, they'd most likely be put down. The shelters are just too full and the pressure too great for the dogs to be on their best behavior in order to be adopted. I hoped the four would survive long enough for me to rehabilitate them so that they too could be off to a new life down the road.

The good news was that Nancy and Melanie were now interested in the big dogs. I couldn't have been happier; I was starting to believe they would live out their days on that godforsaken beach. Yet, I knew their taking the big ones would be a challenge; small dogs and puppies are always the first to be adopted. Bigger dogs and dogs with black or very dark coats are often overlooked.

In the end, most of the remaining dogs from my first day at the beach, the ones that had survived, were on their way to Dr. Ramos's office in San Juan. They still had a long road to recovery, and some wouldn't make it —Lucy, a Dalmatian, died shortly after a surgery to remove a tumor on her heart—but most of them would find their way to real homes. It was the best outcome I could hope for.

TWENTY-SIX

October was good, but this was Dead Dog Beach, so *something* had to go wrong. For all my experience with the dogs and the people who tortured and killed them for sport or convenience, and for all my preparations—I had added a Taser to my self-defense arsenal—some things still took me by surprise.

One morning I drove over to the farthest point of the beach, past the boathouse, to where the fishermen plied their trade. Three men were standing behind their truck at the edge of the rusting corrugated metal breakwater. They were so engrossed in whatever they were doing, they didn't appear to hear or see me as I rolled up to the right of where they were standing. I thought their body language was suspicious, the way they were peering into the turbulent water below. I feared they had thrown one of my dogs into the drink.

I got out of the truck and went to the back to prep the dogs' food and water. I could hear the men laughing and shouting wildly. They sounded drunk. I needed to get closer without startling them.

There was an old shack to my right, and I wandered in that direction, pretending to mind my own business feeding the dogs. When I got a little closer, I could see they each had a crossbow and were shooting at something in the water. They stopped to reload.

I felt a surge of panic and anger. I didn't want to overreact and get myself killed, but I needed to do something fast if one of my dogs was the target.

They continued laughing and shouting as they took aim toward whatever they had in their sights in the water.

"*Hola!*" I said, offering a friendly wave, hoping to distract them. I thought maybe they'd go away once they realized I was there.

I looked toward the water to see what they were aiming at. *Not the manatees!*

"What the hell are you doing?" I shouted, no longer thinking of my own safety. I pulled my Taser from its sheath on my belt and suddenly found myself standing only a few feet from the men, screaming profanities in their faces.

They looked perplexed that this gringo was stupid enough to try to face them down.

One of the men looked angry that I was spoiling their fun. He took a step toward me.

I pressed the trigger of the Taser as a warning, the bright current pulsating and buzzing between the contact points. The man stopped in his tracks.

"Don't even try it, asshole!"

They talked among themselves for a few moments, then put their hands up in a surrender position. Slowly they placed their weapons in the bed of their vehicle, then piled into the truck and sped away. I held my hands over my face to protect against the gravel spraying from the tires.

When they were gone, I walked to the water's edge to look for the manatees. I saw two surface just offshore. Each had several arrows embedded in its flesh, but they were swimming together as a family. It seemed the duo was searching for another. My mind raced back to the time I had been in the water swimming with these beautiful creatures. I was certain they were going to die and there was nothing I could do to help them. There was no cell reception at this part of the beach, and there was no one to call anyway.

CHAPTER TWENTY-SEVEN

S teve McGarva?" a woman's voice said when I answered the phone. "This is Susan Saltaro. I'm a reporter with Univision in San Juan, and I'd like to do a story on you and your dogs."

Finally, news of my work on the beach had made it to someone who could really help, on a big scale.

We arranged a day and time to meet. I was simultaneously nervous and excited. It had been an unbelievably hard year, and I wanted to choose my words wisely during the interview.

I arrived early at the beach that day, spending the morning thinking about what to say and what to leave out so as not to anger my enemies even more than I already had. I didn't want to shame or embarrass anyone into doing the right thing. That never really works anyway. I just hoped that I could show by my example how to treat animals humanely, thereby compelling viewers to do the same thing. The more I thought about it, the more optimistic I became. I wanted the local community to stand up and be proud of the beautiful area where they lived.

Susan and her team showed up right on time.

"Would you like to meet the dogs?" I said.

She and her cameraman followed me around the different areas of the beach where I fed the dogs. We strolled through the boathouse, our shoes crunching the broken glass that still covered the concrete floor. As we walked, I described what had happened to many of the dogs during my time here—the assaults, the dogs that had died protecting me, the poisonings.

"This is one of the saddest things I've ever heard, or seen," she said through tears.

I was glad to hear her say that. It meant she was really getting it.

Everywhere we went that day, the pack followed along, as always, being their lovable selves.

"Are they always this sweet?" she said.

"Always."

"And they always follow you around like this?"

"It's my pack. I'm their alpha." I smiled. "It's hard to believe they've been used and thrown away, isn't it?"

Susan and her camera guy decided to set up in front of the boathouse for the interview. And then she began, asking me questions in English, then translating them into Spanish for her viewers.

"You moved to the island as a visitor from another country. You and your wife have spent a lot of time and your own money trying to clean up a problem that, quite frankly, isn't yours. With everything you've been through in the last year, what message would you like to send to the viewing audience?"

It was a damn good thing I'd prepared myself for a question like this. In my heart, I was pissed off and wanted to trash all the people responsible for the death and mistreatment of so many dogs, but I knew this wasn't the time or place, nor would it help.

"I hope people will feel compelled to take action and do the same thing in their communities that I'm doing here. I want people to realize that they can make a difference. It's always a good choice to help another living creature."

She smiled, urging me to continue.

"And it's contagious! Before you know it, more and more people are doing the right thing to make the world a better place."

When the camera was off, Susan said, "You handled that really well."

"I wanted to put a positive spin on it. I want people to think there is some hope."

As they packed up the news van, Susan said, "Stay in touch, will you? I'd like to hear how things are going here."

I promised I would.

When she was gone, I stood alone with my dogs on this beautiful, godforsaken beach, as on every day before this one. I hoped tomorrow would bring change. I really wanted to believe that this interview would be the big break we'd been hoping for.

I had a strange feeling about it, though. It reminded me of a premonition I'd had years earlier while on a climbing trip, just hours before I witnessed a fellow climber land beside me after falling a thousand feet to his death. Or the day I'd begged my buddy not to fly his paraglider, only to see him lose control moments after launching and hit the ground, his body smashed into pieces before my eyes.

Now, in the back of my mind, I worried that I'd just poked the wasp nest.

The following morning, my senses were screaming at me when I got to the beach. I drove down the long beach road, whistling and calling for the dogs. Where the hell were they?

I pulled up to the metal storage containers where the dogs usually waited for me. I jumped out, calling and whistling, but nothing.

What the hell?

I walked around, calling the dogs' names until, finally, a few of the alphas poked their heads out of the jungle and from hiding places I'd never seen the dogs use before. They were looking over their shoulders as they approached me. They seemed relieved to see me.

Instinctively I switched into damage control mode. I needed to do a head count and see who was missing. The results were devastating. *It can't be this many. They must be hiding somewhere.*

I walked with the pack down the beach along the edge of the jungle. I thought maybe some of the dogs had been scared enough to run toward the hotel. I had become a good tracker during this last year, looking for signs of change or something out of the ordinary. Down here, it could mean the difference between life and death. Now I walked the sand, looking for paw prints, evidence that the dogs had come this way. Nothing.

I turned back toward the boathouse. As I got nearer, the dogs started acting strange again, spooked.

It was always difficult to see inside the boathouse from the outside. My truck was parked on the far left side of the structure near the big side entrance facing the metal containers. I figured I'd cut through and have a look.

I was about twenty paces in when my eyes started to adjust to the dim lighting. I did a slow scan of the giant empty space before me. And then I stopped.

As I squinted across the boat slip, I could make out what looked like a line of dogs hanging from the metal structure along the ceiling. The pack started to bark. This is what they had been trying to tell me all morning.

I faintly heard someone cry, "No!" I struggled to recognize the voice at first, and then I realized it was my own. I was vaguely aware that the pack was still barking, but I couldn't really hear them anymore. They followed me as I ran toward the silhouettes hanging in the distance. I stumbled as my knees grew weak. I slowed to a walk, hardly believing my eyes.

There were deep vertical and diagonal claw marks on the corrugated metal walls next to where my dogs hung by their necks, as though some of them had used their last breaths fighting to get free.

Some of the dogs were lying dead in a pile on the floor. *They must have poisoned these.*

Most of my missing dogs were there, but some remained unaccounted for. My head was spinning.

Suddenly I was back in Canada, a young apprentice at a local automotive shop. I had gone to work early that morning to open up the shop and make coffee for the guys. I walked into the office to find my boss hanging by the neck from the rafters. I'd never forgotten the look on his face.

Back in the present, I struggled to stay on my feet. Finally, I gasped for air, and my head cleared a little. It seems I had forgotten to breathe.

I had crossed over to a dark place in my mind, a place no one really wants to admit exists, but in desperate times you find yourself teetering on the edge and catch a glimpse of the other side. It's a bad place to be.

But I had to stay focused. I didn't want the dogs' bodies to fall and hit the ground as I freed them. I went back outside and got my SUV, backing it into position near the dogs. I climbed on the roof and began cutting them loose. Their bodies were heavier than I expected, and I struggled not to topple off. Over the next two hours, I lowered each one to the ground, and then carried them one by one to the graveyard.

When I was done, I went back to the boathouse to get the truck and drove over to where the dogs lay waiting under the palms. Inside the passenger compartment, the air-conditioning felt good on my overheated body. It sharpened my thinking, but I felt guilty for enjoying this little pleasure while my dogs lay dead in the sand. I shut the engine off and got out to dig.

One of the gardeners from the local hotel drove up alongside me in his little red Isuzu. He would come by from time to time to go fishing with his friends at the end of the road, where I'd seen the manatees shot. He always waved hello as he tootled by. He was one of the men who had warned me about the hotel owners and the police hating the dogs and me. This time, he stopped his truck and leaned out the window, his face resting on his arm. The pack didn't get up or bark.

"You okay, bro?" he asked, his brows furrowed.

I choked back tears. I hadn't seen anyone all day, and I'd kept it together until now.

"Who would do this to my dogs?"

He looked as though he might cry as well. "I don't know. Maybe somebody who see you on TV last night. Everybody in Puerto Rico probably see you last night."

I'd been so excited about getting the word out to the public. "I thought it would help. I didn't say anything bad about anyone. So why would someone do this?"

"They want the dogs gone. They want you gone. Listen, anybody who would do this to dogs will do it to you. You got to be careful. Please, bro."

"I am not a careful man. Not anymore."

"You want help? Nobody should do that alone."

"No thanks, man. I'll do it. You'd better go."

"I am so sorry, my friend," he said, looking at the pile of corpses. "Very bad. They will go to hell for this, I think."

"This is hell."

He mouthed *"I'm sorry"* before driving away. I believed him.

When I was done with my grim task, which took most of the day, I sat by the graves. Twenty-two dogs buried in one day. I hoped the eight that were still missing were all right, but I knew better. I'd find them in a few days when I could smell their decaying remains.

I needed to go home and find a way to sort this horror out in my head. I felt like I was on the edge of losing it. Pam was constantly worried about me now. I suppose she had every reason to be. Most days I would downplay most of the crazy things that happened, to spare her the added concern. Sometimes I called her to tell her what had happened, but she'd be busy or have a meeting. I might try to call my brother Barry or my mum, but they weren't here, and didn't really understand what I was going through. And always, when I hung up, I was alone with my thoughts. Pam knew that when the days were especially bad, I might have a shot of whiskey earlier than normal, by myself. She was stuck at work and couldn't do anything to help, or to stop me. But ultimately she trusted me, and she prayed my drinking wouldn't become a real problem.

It was the first time I seriously thought about quitting. All I had ever wanted was to save the dogs, but now they were dying *because* of me. It was a new low.

TWENTY-EIGHT

The next day the dogs were still a bit off. They avoided the boathouse and got pretty jumpy whenever a vehicle drove up to the beach. I was on edge too.

I grabbed my Taser, machete, and billy club to bring with me as I walked around. There were still dogs missing, and I couldn't rest until I found them. I decided to walk up an isolated dead-end road where some of the dogs had turned up in the past. It was eerily quiet as I went. It was still early, and the sea breeze was just beginning to kick up. I couldn't smell anything . . . yet. And then I reached a spot where the dogs stopped following me. I knew I'd better investigate.

I continued along to where one of the big black Labs had given birth to her puppies a couple of months earlier. I hadn't patrolled this area on a regular basis since Mary had taken the pups to her house a few weeks ago.

I rounded the corner and looked up. One of my dogs was hanging by the neck from a tree. His feet were tied with gauze, and tattered bed sheets served as his noose. Whoever did this had burned the dog after they hung him.

I calmly walked around him, still numb from yesterday. I figured the other missing dogs must be near.

I wasn't able to reach high enough to cut him down, so I grabbed a shipping pallet that lay at the base of the tree to stand on. The dog had probably been there for at least thirty-six hours; it was already decomposing. Up close the smell was almost too much to bear.

I struggled to keep my balance as I strained to reach high enough to cut the bed sheet with my machete in my right hand, using my left to support the dog. When the material finally gave way, the weight of the dog was too much, and I lost my footing. Next thing I knew, we were both falling through the air. I hit the pallet on my side, which knocked the wind out of me. I rolled off to the ground. I was dazed, holding my ribs, trying to catch my breath. I looked over to my left and screamed. The dead dog was in a heap right next to me.

I scrambled to my feet and backed away in a frenzy, as though I'd never seen or touched a corpse. I started to cry when I realized that I'd dropped the dog's body.

The dogs were going nuts barking. I must have startled them when I fell.

"Shut up!" I shouted to quiet them, something I had never done before.

I was really rattled. I wasn't sure I'd recover from this one. As I slowly made my way back to the truck, I was hurting in more ways than one. I needed to bury this poor boy.

I had to do something with the maelstrom of emotions swirling inside me. I needed to talk to someone who understood.

I called Melanie, hoping she might be able to think more clearly than I was and come up with a new game plan. My call went immediately to voice mail.

I tried Nancy. Voice mail.

I was furious with them for not answering, although they had already warned me that they had started screening my calls because they found the stories I told them too depressing.

"What do you think it's like for me and the dogs, living those horror stories every day?" I'd said.

I knew it wasn't fair of me to be angry, but I needed them. So much for that.

I spent the rest of the day sitting in the shade of a palm tree (safely out of the trajectory of any falling coconuts). It was obvious to me that whoever had committed this massacre was sending a message, one I received loud and clear: they wanted me to stop. *I don't care. I won't quit. They picked the wrong guy to mess with.*

I fell asleep with the remaining pack, about forty-five dogs now. But that number would grow again as more dogs were dumped daily.

I was nudged awake by the sound of whimpering, a wet nose pressed against my skin. I looked at the concerned faces of my dogs and realized that, no matter how out of control things seemed, this was the most fulfilled I'd felt in years. These dogs were willing to die for me. And I was willing to die for them too.

Nancy returned my call the next morning.

"Steve, I'm going to put you on speaker. Melanie is with me." They were on their way to a yoga class. "What's up?"

I felt dead inside. I was still angry they hadn't called back the day before when I needed support. I told them briefly what had happened over the previous two days, which dogs were dead, which were still unaccounted for. When I was done speaking, the only sound to break the silence was Nancy's bawling in the background. I had nothing more to say.

"Steve, you should stay away from the beach for a while," Melanie finally said. "Let things settle down."

Easy for her to say. She didn't know my dogs or care about them the way I did.

"We've got a connection at the San Juan Police Department," she went on. "We'll give him a call. Maybe we can hire a private investigator to stake out the beach."

In the background, I heard Nancy say, "We should get some surveillance equipment, set up cameras all over the boathouse and the beach."

"How the hell are you going to manage that?" I said. I knew they were trying to make me feel better, but all I felt was disappointment. Desperate for something to ease the strain I was feeling, I decided to go paragliding. Whenever I felt I wasn't coping very well, I headed to the central mountains to go flying. Flying always balanced me out, and I needed to settle my thoughts and get a bigger perspective.

It was an amazing day. I flew harder and maybe a little crazier than normal, but I was feeling good again as I swooped and spiraled over the lush valley below. As the sun dipped down in the western sky, I landed between the horses and cows standing peacefully in the field near where I'd parked my truck, packed up my gear, and headed for home. Usually I'd feel a high from the experience that would last the rest of the day, drift into a peaceful night's sleep, and wake jazzed the next morning. Not this time. From the moment I got behind the wheel, I found myself driving aggressively the whole way back to Palmas del Mar. I arrived home feeling bothered, out of sorts. My thoughts went round and round, like a dog chasing its tail.

I sat out by the pool with a bottle of scotch and "drank about it" until Pam got home.

"How are you doing?" she asked. Obviously it was a rhetorical question. She could see on my face that I was struggling.

"Would you like something to eat?" she tried again.

I wasn't hungry. I just wanted to drink tonight.

Pam made herself a salad and sat down to do some work, while I stewed over my thoughts. I gazed at the reflection of the moon on the surface of the water and listened to the call of the coqui. If someone had walked into our lives at that moment, it would all seem too perfect. We were living on a tropical island in the Caribbean in a beautiful house, sipping mojitos by the pool. But it's very different living in a foreign country than it is visiting on vacation and staying at an all-inclusive resort. Many of the other expat families we knew were struggling too. The reasons were different, but that didn't really matter. The others all seemed to be in denial about how they felt. Whenever Pam and I would try to talk about our personal experiences and the challenges we were facing, the other expats would dismiss us, declaring how much they loved living there. They made us feel like we were alone in our unhappiness. But we knew we weren't alone; it just appeared that way.

I felt like I would smack the next person who equated our expat life to "being permanently on holiday." They had no idea.

When we decided to take the leap and move to Puerto Rico, we knew there would be some obvious hurdles to jump: finding a house, getting a car, figuring out where to get groceries and supplies, that kind of thing. These are the hassles of everyday life that back home we knew how to handle. But working out new systems and processes was only the half of it when you have a different language and culture to contend with as well.

Generally one person puts his or her life on hold in order to live abroad as well. When a spouse is given an overseas assignment, the partner is faced with many obstacles that are often ignored. Unfortunately, the company didn't offer support for trailing spouses. We thought I would be able to get a job and work part-time somewhere to socialize and make friends, but we quickly found out that it was a near impossibility. We assumed that Internet access would be easily available to maintain contact with friends and family back home, only to discover that it takes months to get connected and it only works intermittently.

Many of our friends and relatives back home deemed our life exotic, seeing only the positives: the nice homes, the exciting travel experiences. They would visit and see our "new lifestyle" through holiday-tinted lenses. They saw us as fortunate and capable, but what they didn't see was that often the experience felt a bit like the old duck analogy—giving the impression that everything was calm and under control on the surface, while just beneath the surface we were paddling like mad just to keep afloat.

TWENTY-NINE

I woke up with a hangover from too many glasses of scotch, but I wasn't going to let that stop me from going to the beach. I'd never missed a day, and I wasn't going to start now.

I started the morning with the dogs at the storage containers, feeding and hanging out with them for about an hour before moving on to other areas of the beach. Most of the surviving dogs were present, but a few new ones were staying to themselves near the jetty, so I jumped into my truck for the short drive over to the point. I drove slowly, with the door open and my foot resting on the running board, so I could talk to the dogs as they followed alongside.

As I rounded the corner and pulled into the gravel parking lot, I scanned for newcomers. Off to the left, at the far end of the parking lot, I saw a guy backing his boat and trailer down the dirt ramp into the water. Several other men were standing around watching. When I got nearer, I saw they had cornered a couple of my dogs between the breakwater and the boat ramp. They were having a big laugh taunting the animals, acting tough like they were lion tamers instead of jerks picking on defenseless, friendly dogs.

Whenever I'd seen guys down here before, usually drunk, they tended to scatter when I showed up, but this lot was making so much noise they didn't hear me approach. The dogs that had followed me were visibly upset. Some had fallen back and started to bark.

I stopped the truck and got out just as one of the men reached into the bed of their pickup and pulled out a container of gasoline. Maybe it's for the boat, I thought. But he wasn't walking toward the boat. He was going toward the dogs they'd corralled. Before I could make a move, the man had doused the dogs with gasoline.

One of the dogs tried to make a break for it, bolting between the men's legs. He got through but not before getting his ribs kicked in. His terrified yelp caused my dogs to ratchet up the barking. He tumbled across the gravel, then got up and ran like hell. He never looked back.

The men were whooping and hollering, taunting the dog they still had trapped between them, completely unaware of my presence. The dog was cowering, his head down and his tail between his legs, his whole body shaking. He tried to run, but the men kept scaring him back. The man with the container lunged toward the dog.

"No!" I screamed.

The gasoline sprayed through the air, drenching the dog's body.

The men roared with laughter as another man flicked a match toward the dog.

The dog burst into flames. The men skittered out of the dog's way as it thrashed around, falling down, smashing into everything in his path. The dog's cries of pain were unlike anything I'd ever heard. Adrenaline surged through me. I was filled with pure, white-hot rage.

The next thing I knew, I was running full speed toward the men. I slammed into the back of the man holding the gas can with my fists and elbows, knocking him to the ground. His head whipped back like he'd been hit by a car, as I stumbled over him into the middle of the group.

I drew my machete before they understood what had just happened. Everything went quiet except for the sound of the screaming dog in the background and my heart beating like a war drum in my head.

I maneuvered out of the circle and started backing toward my truck, the dogs keeping them at bay so I could get a safe distance away. There was no room for mistakes now. I knew they'd likely kill me if they got hold of me.

The guy I'd knocked down got up. He made a move as if to get around behind me. I pointed the machete toward him.

"Don't even try it, you piece of shit! I'll kill you where you stand!"

In all likelihood, he didn't understand what I said, but it didn't matter. He stopped in his tracks and put his hands up in front of him in a gesture of surrender. They all took a few steps back.

I was terrified. I felt surges of panic trying to take over. I had to convince them I was crazier than they were. Maybe I was. What the hell was I thinking? I hadn't even helped the poor dog, which lay twitching and dying in the gravel fifty feet from where I stood. And now I'd put the rest of the dogs and myself in danger. *I'm so stupid.*

I bumped into the front of my truck. The driver's side door was still open. I slipped in and started the engine. The dogs disappeared into the jungle.

This felt all too familiar, like a recycled dream. I flashed back to Kyle and the others lying dead in the gravel a few short months ago. Once again, my dogs had stayed by my side and protected me.

I felt a nudge on my arm. It was Scampi, one of the first dogs I'd discovered at this beach a year ago. She must have jumped into the truck during the commotion. She was sitting on the passenger seat, whimpering and shaking like a leaf in the wind. I'd heard her bark during the confrontation—she had a strained, raspy bark that made me think she must have been kicked in the throat before I met her. She reminded me of a dog my dad had brought home from the pound for me when I was a little boy. I had named him Scamp, and I loved him more than anyone thought possible. Scampi and I had gotten close when I nursed her back to health after she'd eaten something that caused her temporary paralysis and she almost died. She had defended me one day, getting her ribs kicked in while chasing away guys looking to start a fight.

I sat staring at the men through the windshield for a long moment before deciding it would be best to back the truck up and leave. The men looked relieved to see me pull away. I was scared to death, but I must have scared them more. I didn't feel triumphant.

I drove toward the end of the jungle on the other side of the beach where

I knew the other dogs would be hiding. I was out of sight of the men for now, but I needed to hurry up and get the hell out of there. The dogs had an intricate maze of places to hide in the jungle, so I knew they'd be safe for the time being.

I pulled over and got out of the truck. Scampi needed to be with the pack. I felt horrible when I opened the passenger side door. She didn't want to get out. I picked her up and shut the door behind me with my foot. If I didn't, she'd try to get back in. I set her down on the sand. Her eyes locked onto mine. God, I loved this dog. How could I do this to her? We weren't allowed to have dogs at the house we were renting. We'd be evicted, for sure. Our landlady had a caretaker who watched everything we did and reported back to her. I held Scampi's face as I told her, "I'll be back for you. I'll get you off this beach if it's the last thing I do. You just have to hold on a little longer, sweetie. Please don't give up."

Once again, I found myself crying as I drove away.

That evening I called Nancy to tell her what had happened. I got her voice mail. I tried Melanie. Voice mail. Then Martha. Voice mail.

What else was new?

My rage was spilling into the rest of my life. The morning after the dog was torched, Pam and I were talking once again about how I needed to be more careful.

"Steve, I'm serious. I better not get a call telling me you're dead," Pam said, with a new sternness I hadn't heard before.

I promised I'd try to rein myself in.

I exited the freeway in Juncos and was making my way through town when I had to slam on the brakes at an intersection to avoid hitting a car that ran a stoplight. It was a close call. And then all of a sudden a guy pulled a slingshot maneuver to get past me on my left, but he didn't have enough room because of oncoming traffic so he lurched back into my lane. I had to crank the wheel to the right and step on it to avoid being sideswiped as he pulled in front of me.

I felt my blood boil. I honked the horn and flipped him off. He punched his brakes, nearly causing me to bump into the back of his car. I honked again. This time, he gave me the finger. Without a thought, up came mine as well.

"Steve, you're making a big deal out of nothing. Calm down," Pam said from the passenger seat next to me.

"He started it! He nearly hit us!"

The offending car had pulled into the left lane, and I started pulling into the right lane to make the turn. As I did, the car swerved into my lane again. I blared the horn and screamed.

"Stephen! Leave it alone!"

"I just want to drive you to work, Pammie. How is this my fault?"

I jockeyed for position until I was side by side with the other car, which was slowly edging closer in the dense traffic. He was going to scrape right by me if I didn't get out of his way, but I had nowhere to go. I felt twinges of fight-or-flight coursing through me. Pam was still telling me to take it easy, but I wasn't really listening anymore.

"Stop lecturing me! I'm going to let him pass, okay?"

As the traffic began to move, the car moved over to the left again. The moment had passed. I started rolling forward in the right lane and I'll be damned if he didn't try to move over into my lane again. I lost it. I leaned on the horn and didn't let up until the driver got out of his car. He put his hands on the roof of his car and screamed at me in Spanish. I kept on the horn. I guess he didn't like that. He reached into the back of his car and pulled something out. He started walking around his car toward me. That's when I caught a glimpse of his machete. Before Pam could stop me, I was out of the truck with my own machete in my hand.

"You really want to mess with me, dude? Come on!"

He stopped in his tracks.

When I turned to get back in the truck, I looked quickly over my shoulder and saw that he was coming after me.

"Get in the truck, Stephen!" Pam yelled.

I shut the door. I wanted to stop him before he came any closer. I moved toward him until he retreated to his car. When I jumped back in the truck, Pam was furious.

I started to roll forward, and this driver aggressively cut in front of me again. I steered up alongside, reached out my window with the machete, and whacked the roof of his car. It made a hell of a sound and probably a hell of a dent.

He stopped and jumped out of his car again. I did the same. He looked startled that I wasn't backing down. He screamed at me and swung his machete through the air.

"Enough!" I yelled, and slammed the machete edge down onto the back of his car. There was a loud pop as beads of safety glass flew from the rear window. The man looked stunned. I hit his car again on the trunk and gestured as though I was coming for him next. He finally got back in his car and pulled away.

I was standing in the middle of the street in a very rough town with a machete in my hand, having just had a major confrontation with a guy who probably lived here. Reality kicked in.

I got back in the truck, put it in gear, and stepped on it. Just when I thought I'd lost the guy, I saw him a few cars back chasing us down in the middle of the road.

The gate at the entrance to the manufacturing plant closed behind us just as he pulled up.

As Pam got out, I said very little. "Bye. Love you."

"You're out of control, Stephen. Are you going to be all right?" I knew she was pissed at me for losing my temper but keeping it to herself for now.

I slinked out the gates looking carefully in both directions before proceeding back out to the streets of Juncos. I drove the rest of the way home wondering if I'd be killed because of a stupid traffic dispute. I was definitely losing my grip. I needed to settle down and clear my head. But I knew the dogs were waiting for me.

CHAPTER THIRTY-ONE

T hey're shooting the dogs," I said to Pam a few weeks later.
I'd been finding CO_2 cartridges in the sand, and the dogs were turning up with splotches of paint on them. Someone was using them as paintball targets. When I tried to clean the paint off their tender skin, the dogs would wince and whimper in pain. Up close, I could see that the spots where they'd been hit were swollen and red.

Then I noticed that some of the dogs had what appeared to be infected insect bites on their necks, scalps, and other areas of their bodies. They could hardly sit still, twitching and gnawing at themselves. On closer inspection, it looked like ticks had burrowed under their skin. I managed to get one dog to hold still long enough to let me investigate. I picked and squeezed at the angry bump until a silver pellet popped out. Someone was shooting at the dogs with lead pellets from an air rifle too.

Whoever was behind this was upping the ante. A few weeks later I started seeing entry and exit wounds on the dogs' legs and shoulders. I found .22-caliber shells on the ground near the boathouse.

Over time the dogs had learned that the food I put out for them was the only safe food, and they avoided food put out by strangers at the beach. I was grateful for this, since it made life a little less perilous for them.

But they didn't stand a chance against a bullet.

Day after day, week after week, I had become hyperaware of imminent danger, to the point where I looked for it even when it didn't exist. So it came as a complete shock when danger came barreling at me from something as mundane as a toothache.

An old filling had been acting up, but with everything else going on, I just learned to live with the ache and chew on the other side of my mouth. Then, one Friday afternoon, I bit a piece of ice and a sharp pain tore through my jaw.

I tried to ignore it over the weekend, hoping the pain would subside, but by Monday morning I was in agony and I decided to go see the local doctor at the shopping center in Palmas del Mar. He seemed like a nice guy. During the preliminary small talk, he told me that he was originally from the States but had moved to the island after medical school to be near his family.

He took a look at the tooth and felt the glands in my neck.

"There could be an infection in the root. We need to do something before it gets any worse." He made a joke about the local hospitals as he wrote me a prescription for antibiotics and a painkiller. "Call me if the pain doesn't get better."

Tuesday night I was standing at our barbecue grill making supper when the skin between my fingers and toes suddenly became so itchy I couldn't stand it.

"Maybe it's an allergy to the grass in the backyard?" Pam suggested. I'd washed and folded my kite-surfing gear on the lawn earlier in the day. "Why don't you jump in the pool?"

She didn't have to ask twice. The swim helped.

We ate dinner and relaxed with a glass of wine by the pool. We had family coming to visit in a few days, and we were pretty excited, making plans for the upcoming holidays with them. My brother Barry, my mum, my stepdad, Blair, my daughter, Bethany, and her boyfriend Ryan were all on their way. Finally, we had something to look forward to.

While we were sitting there, I noticed my fingers and toes starting to itch again. Now the roof of my mouth and the inside of my ears joined in.

"Try another swim?" Pam said.

It was late, and I was getting tired. I had to do something to calm my skin or I'd never get any sleep. I took her advice and then hit the hay. I was out cold in no time.

I woke up around 1 A.M. to go to the bathroom. The itch was back, and the soles of my feet were uncomfortable now. Back in bed, I couldn't get comfortable and drifted in and out of sleep. I lost track of time.

At some point during the night, I was dimly aware of something lying on my face, like a pillow. I reached up to remove whatever the hell it was. When my hand touched my cheek, I jolted awake. *What the hell?* I couldn't open my eyes. They were swollen and sealed shut. My hand against my face felt like water balloons touching.

Fear and panic flooded over me. I was wide awake now. I did a quick assessment of my body. My hands and arms were hugely swollen and puffy. My feet and legs were the same. I couldn't tell if my face was swollen, because I couldn't feel properly with my hands. I couldn't see, and my ears were filled with a ringing sound.

I lay there, trying to calm down, but then I started to have trouble breathing. *I'm in trouble.*

I reached over to shake Pam awake, but she was unmovable. I tried to speak, but my tongue and lips were like bratwurst sausages. I shook her again, more aggressively this time.

"What are you doing? I'm trying to sleep!" she grumbled, rolling away from me.

"Pammie, I need to get to the hospital. Something's wrong," I said as calmly as I could. I felt bad for waking her up and didn't want to freak her out. It was probably a false alarm and I was going to look like an idiot for overreacting.

Half awake, Pam was on autopilot when she slid out of bed and made her way to the shower without looking at me, and I was too preoccupied with fear to even think of telling her to skip the ablutions. It seemed like an eternity passed while she was in there. My breathing became more labored. I got out of bed to see how much longer Pam would be, but my feet were so swollen now it was painful to walk. I crawled to the bathroom.

When the shower shut off, I called out, "Pammie!"

She opened the door and looked down at me sitting on the floor. Panic swept over her face. "Oh my God! You look really bad, Steve."

"I told you I need to go to the hospital," I said, annoyed that she had taken so much time to get ready. Did she think I was kidding?

"Can you get yourself dressed and downstairs?" she said, kicking into high gear. "I'll be ready in a minute and I'll help you out to the truck."

While she finished getting ready, I got myself downstairs. She came flying after me in a frenzy of disorganized thinking.

"I don't even know where the hospital is!" she said in full panic mode.

"Let's just head toward San Juan and follow the hospital signs on the freeway."

After a hair-raising drive in what turned into rush hour traffic, we finally found the correct exit for the hospital. We had tried to call a couple of our ex-pat acquaintances to see if anyone had proper directions, but my fingers were too swollen to punch the keys on the cell phone, and Pam was too frazzled by the driving to be of much help.

And then we had to wait endlessly in the emergency ward to see someone, first in the waiting room, then in a dingy back hallway. I was covered with a rash and running a fever now, and the air-conditioning was cranked so high that I was freezing.

Finally, a doctor came to take my blood pressure.

"Why are you so swollen?" he asked.

"That's why we're here. We were hoping *you* could tell *us*." Pam gave him the background about my tooth. "He's taking penicillin, but he's missed a dose."

The doctor looked at me, perplexed. "Go ahead and take the next pill. I have no idea what's causing these symptoms, but I'd like to keep your husband for observation." He ordered Benadryl and an IV and said he'd back to check on me later. A nurse found a wheelchair for me until a bed could be made available. The medicine made me groggy and I drifted in and out of sleep.

We waited the entire day for the doctor to come back.

"You're looking much better," he said. "How do you feel?"

The only obvious improvement was that I was breathing a bit better.

"Great. You can go home."

"Really?" Pam asked, incredulous.

"Yep, you're good to go. We really don't know what's causing this rash, but you'll be more comfortable at home."

I went straight to bed as soon as we got home that evening. Pam came in a few hours later to give me the penicillin for my tooth. I fell right back to sleep.

I woke at 4 A.M. It took only a light touch from me to wake Pam up this time.

I managed to mumble the words, "I need to go back to the hospital. Now!"

When we got to the emergency ward, we were greeted by the same staff as on the previous morning. "What are you doing here?" the doctor asked, looking genuinely puzzled.

Are you serious? Just look at me!

He ordered another IV of whatever he'd given me the day before and left to do rounds.

One of the perks of Pam's job was the relocation services that the company provided to expat employees. While I slept, Pam made calls, and in a short while we had one of the relocation services gals at the hospital to help us navigate their medical system. While she battled with the doctors to have a specialist come look at me, Pam called my family to let them know what was going on.

At some point during the day, after a call from Pam, the company's on-site nurse drove up from Juncos to have a look at me. As soon as she did, she too joined the fight to get a specialist in to see me.

Finally, around 5 P.M., an internal medicine specialist turned up wondering what all the fuss was about. The company nurse filled him in as he examined me.

"This is obviously a reaction to the penicillin," he explained to Pam, a concerned look on his face. "I'm frankly surprised that the doctor you saw yesterday suggested your husband keep taking it. It very well could have killed him."

He instructed one of the nurses to find me a room. I was going to be admitted. "I'm afraid your husband is not out of the woods yet," he said to Pam. He told her she'd need to get some bedding for me; the hospital couldn't provide such luxuries as sheets, blankets, and pillows.

Pam leaned over my bed and kissed me before she went home. "Get some rest. I'll be back in a few hours." I dozed off before she was out the door

I woke up in a dimly lit room with no idea where I was or how long I'd been there. Something was wrong. I could hear a group of women talking and laughing on the other side of the curtain surrounding my bed. I tried to reach the call button but it was just out of reach. I tried to reposition myself better, and stretched as far as I could. I almost had it in my grasp when I suddenly became light-headed and passed out.

When I came to, there was still no one there. I thought I had pushed the button but I guess I hadn't. My swollen tongue was filling my mouth now, and I was unable to call out. Or breathe. I tried desperately to push the call button. I had no idea if I was doing it or not. I passed out again.

When I came to again, I heard the sound of the curtain opening and a nurse saying something in Spanish. Through the narrow window of my swollen eyelids, I could see her look at me, then calmly turn and walk away.

This is how I'm going to die?

I lay there quietly, trying to concentrate on getting a little air past the swelling in my mouth and throat. I tried to meditate to calm down. It seemed to help a little. I wasn't scared anymore, just sad. I always figured I'd go out in some freak climbing accident or in a paragliding crash, not suffocating because of a stupid allergic reaction to a common drug. What a bummer.

I started thinking about how sad all the people who loved me were going to be. I knew Pam would blame herself for not being with me when I died. I hated to think of how much pain she would have to face. She had always been there for me, supporting my crazy way of approaching life and still loving me.

Through all the chaos, I'd almost forgotten that my family was coming. Barry was due to arrive tomorrow, Mum and Blair the following day, Bethany and Ryan the day after that. They would be devastated. Some Christmas this was going to be.

I was sad that my relationship with my brother Ian had been strained of late and that we hadn't talked in over a year. Now I would never have a chance to make things right with him. I knew he'd carry the guilt forever and I hated the thought of it.

I had just managed to restore my relationship with Bethany, but I hadn't had the chance to do the same with her brother, Curtis. I worried about how they would handle my death.

But mostly I was calm. I was at peace with dying. It was different than I'd imagined. I had no sense of time anymore. I felt my body involuntarily trying to get air into my lungs, my heart trying to keep the beat. But I was drifting off, becoming less and less aware. I was too weak, too tired. My body was giving in.

"Steve! Steve! Wake up!"

I could barely make out Pam's voice through the swelling in my ears.

"Help me!" I heard her scream.

It made me feel better that she would at least be able to say good-bye to me. I tried to open my eyes to look at her one last time, but I could only make out a blurry figure. The backlighting made her appear angelic.

"My husband can't breathe!" she screamed at the nurses as she ripped open the curtain around my bed.

One of the nurses ambled over and looked in at me. "What's the problem?"

"He can't breathe! He's dying!" Pam said.

"Wasn't he like this before?"

"Do something! Help him!"

I heard the nurse call for assistance. Within moments, I had more attention than I'd had in two days. I passed out.

"I'm sorry I left you, sweetheart," Pam was saying through tears when I came to. "I love you."

Apparently the nurses had forgotten to give me my medicine, and Pam had caught it just in time. Apparently it wasn't just bedding that family was responsible for; getting the nurses to give out medication was also up to relatives.

Pam climbed into the bed beside me and held me in her arms. I felt her body tremble as she quietly cried herself to sleep.

Around 2 A.M., a nurse woke us up. They'd finally found a room for me. I wondered how one became available at this time of night. Did someone die?

In the morning, Pam left for a little while to find breakfast for me (apparently I'd checked in too late to make the list). She wasn't gone long before I started to have breathing problems again. My throat began to close up again, my tongue to swell. My hands and feet were starting to fill up with fluid. I reached for the call button and pressed it over and over until someone answered. The voice sounded angry.

"Help me. . . . I can't breathe."

I didn't understand her response, but she sounded frustrated and impatient.

The symptoms were coming on stronger and faster this time. That sense that I was going to die returned.

Pam walked into the room, took one look at me, and dropped the bag of food. She bolted for the nurses' station to beg someone to help. Once again, she saved my life in the nick of time. Once gain, the nurses had forgotten to give me my medication.

My mum called Pam's cell phone asking to speak to me. I shook her off. I felt awful and didn't want to talk.

"Put the phone to his ear!" my mother insisted.

Pam did, and it was good that I could reassure my mum with the sound of my voice. She was terrified that I was going to die before she could get there.

"We want you around for Christmas, kiddo," she said.

I wasn't feeling too good about being in that hospital either. I'd survived another day there, but just barely.

The doctor who had seen me in the emergency ward the previous night came by around lunchtime.

"How are you feeling today?"

Pam told him about the missed medication last night and this morning. He wasn't happy.

"I'm concerned about how much swelling you have," he said as he examined the rash now covering my entire body. My whole body looked like I'd been beaten with a baseball bat. "You must have fallen out of bed when you tried to call the nurse."

"He didn't," Pam insisted. "The nurses didn't give him his medication. Every time he goes into anaphylactic shock, he gets worse."

"Hmmm. I'd like to get a CT scan to rule out head trauma, just to be safe."

A short while later, I was plunked into a wheelchair and taken downstairs to another floor, where a nurse parked me in a hallway. I sat there for hours with several other patients who were waiting. An elderly woman who was in line ahead of me reached out her hand and placed it on my arm. She said a few words in Spanish I couldn't understand, but the look of concern on her face said it all. Another patient smiled at me and said the woman was praying for me. I tried to smile in thanks, but I'm sure the result was pretty hideous to look at.

When a technician approached the old woman to tell her they were ready for her to go in, she said something to him and pointed at me.

"Okay," the technician said. He turned to me and smiled. "You're next, my friend. She gave you her place in line."

Pam and I thanked her over and over again as I was wheeled away. She was still waiting when my test was finished, holding a rosary in her hands. She smiled at me and touched my arm as I went past. I never saw her again, but I would never forget her generosity and kindness when I needed it most.

Pam stayed with me in my room that night, but neither of us got any sleep. The gentleman in the next bed was screaming in pain and vomiting into the wee hours. We were pretty sure another bed was about to free up quite soon.

By morning, I was done with this hell. They had nearly killed me twice already, and I was getting more and more run-down from lack of sleep. Pam was still fighting with the nurses to get my medication to me on time.

"I'm checking out of here," I told the doctor who came around after breakfast.

"That's not a good idea," he said.

"Staying here isn't a good idea either. I'm leaving."

"I suppose it's your choice, but I wouldn't advise it."

"I'm going."

"I won't be able to give you any more medication if you leave. The anaphylaxis will probably be even worse next time. You could die if you don't have the correct steroid dose and Benadryl combination."

"But you won't prescribe that for me?"

"No, I'm sorry, sir, if you leave the hospital, you're on your own. You'll have to sign papers releasing the hospital from liability if anything happens to you."

I left anyway. I figured I had a better chance of survival at home.

When we got back to the house, Barry was there. I was so happy to see him. He'd come by the hospital briefly the night before just after he arrived, but I barely remembered his visit.

Meanwhile, Pam did a little Internet research to see if the medication the first doctor had given me might work. She discovered that the drug was exactly the steroid I needed, but with a different name. The directions on the bottle made it clear that I'd need to be weaned off the drugs over the next ten days. Pam calculated that we had just enough to get me through provided we had no setbacks.

I was weak and exhausted, so I went to bed to get some rest, while Pam and Barry went to the airport to pick up my mum and Blair. I woke up that evening to my mum's smiling face. Mum has always believed in me and shown support for every dream I've ever pursued. I know I caused her to worry endlessly with my need to travel the world at a young age, but she encouraged me to follow my heart. I was overwhelmed with gratitude to have her with me now.

"How are you feeling, kiddo?"

Immediately, I started to cry. It was just like when I was a kid and got hurt. I acted tough until I saw my mum, and then the waterworks started.

Over the next couple of weeks, I spent a lot of time in the pool, trying to quell the itching that still plagued me. I still went to the beach, but for shorter amounts of time. I had a hell of a time controlling my emotions. I would be laughing and having a good time with everyone one minute, then sobbing the next. Pam went back to the Internet where she learned that the mood swings were normal for someone weaning off steroids. My family was wonderful about ignoring my intense behavior. They knew I'd get over it. I wasn't sure. I'd never felt so out of control in my life.

There *was* an upside to this unexpected illness. Sometimes when my emotions got the better of me, I excused myself from the family activities to work on my art portfolio, which I needed to put together for my application to the Rhode Island School of Design. I hoped I'd be able to go there when Pam's contract was up and we left the island. The deadline was fast approaching, and I was up against some of the best up-and-coming artists in the world. I needed to put my best foot forward if I was going to stand a chance of getting in. I had planned to have my drawings completed before my family arrived for the holidays, but clearly that plan had been squashed.

I'd been working on one of the drawings for a couple of days, but I wasn't feeling well that morning, so I set the drawing board against the wall under the louvered windows with plans to get back to it that afternoon, after Pam and I took my family on an outing to Old San Juan.

On the drive home, I noticed a band of threatening clouds heading our way.

"Yikes, that looks ominous," Pam said. "Did you all shut your bedroom windows before we left the house?"

I squinted my eyes in thought. I remembered opening the window in my studio to let some light in while I was working. I didn't remember shutting it. "Aw, shit," I said out loud.

Everyone looked at me.

"The window above my drawings. It's open."

I floored it, hoping to get back to the house before the storm struck. No such luck. I raced into the house to find one drawing I'd spent days on ruined.

"Maybe it'll be okay when it dries," my mum said.

I tore it to pieces and threw it in the garbage.

I went upstairs and lay on the cool tiles of the bathroom floor, trying to soothe my irritated skin and my frayed nerves. While I was lying there, frustrated and angry in the knowledge that I'd have to start another drawing soon if I was going to make my deadline, inspiration struck.

There it is. The drawing.

It was like a light went on in my mind. I would draw the bathroom from my perspective on the floor.

Believing that things happen for a reason, I started to draw with renewed energy. Whenever I needed to peel away from company or I wasn't feeling well, I'd go lie on the bathroom floor and draw. Before too long, the drawing was done and I was on to the next. By the end of the holidays, my portfolio was ready to send to RISD.

THIRTY-TWO

After weeks of silence, Melanie Shapiro and Nancy Guilford resurfaced.

"We heard that Susan Saltaro from Univision is coming down to do a follow-up report," Melanie said in an early-morning phone call. "Nancy and I will be there with bells on."

The morning of the interview, they showed up bright and early—unusual for them.

I did my best to ignore them both while Susan and the cameraman set up and miked me for the interview. When we were ready, I started telling Susan what had happened with the dogs since the last time she'd visited the beach. Then, out of nowhere, Nancy stepped directly in front of me and started talking to the reporter. Fortunately, it wasn't live, and Susan was able to change gears like a pro. She started interviewing Nancy without missing a beat.

I always said my work at the beach was all about the dogs, so I chose to bow out and let Nancy have the spotlight. But I couldn't help feeling annoyed and hurt at the way Nancy had commandeered the interview.

The piece aired that evening and again the following morning. I drove to the beach worried about a repeat of what had happened last time. I still wanted to believe that exposing the problem in the community would somehow persuade someone to hold accountable the people responsible. The memory of those dogs strung up in the boathouse was still vivid.

When I pulled up, the dogs were their normal, happy selves. I breathed a sigh of relief.

I spent the morning working on obedience training with my pack. Most of the dogs would sit and lie down on command. But almost all my commands were nonverbal. I figured dogs communicate with one another nonverbally—they read one another's energy, they don't converse. Besides, I didn't want to shout over the sound of fifty barking dogs, or draw unnecessary attention if there was a time I needed them to be quiet. At the beginning, I taught the dogs with a combination of voice commands and hand gestures, but I'd wean them off the voice commands as soon as possible. Once I'd gotten the alpha dog to follow my lead, the other dogs, one by one, fell in line. Eventually the majority of the pack was fully in tune with me and my every move.

I was so proud of my dogs. They had come such a long way since I'd found this place. I was feeling better, so I decided to celebrate and spend the afternoon paragliding with my friend Luca. Catching thermals high enough to see as far as San Juan and the neighboring islands put everything in perspective.

That evening when I picked Pam up from work, she was thrilled to see me happy for a change. Of course, it didn't last.

On the drive to the beach the following morning, I had a bad feeling. I kept having a sense of déjà vu. On the approach road, I slowed down and scanned the jungle on either side looking for anything out of the ordinary. I spotted a pile of plastic garbage bags. They weren't there yesterday. *Shit.*

I pulled up to see if it was just someone's household garbage. I could taste the smell of rotting flesh as I got out of the truck.

I pulled my machete from my side and split open one of the bags. I gagged as a wave of putrid air assaulted my senses. I tore the bag open a bit more and confirmed that it was indeed one of my dogs, a young mother who was a newcomer to the beach. She always had her three pups at her side. I cut the bag all the way open. The pups were there too. Someone had smashed in their skulls. The mom had a gaping wound on her neck.

I felt sick to my stomach. I had to keep it together to find out what was in the rest of the bags. I cut open the second bag and found two more mutilated dogs inside. The third and fourth bags were the same. Ten dogs dead.

I got the plastic tarp out of the back of the truck and slid the bags onto it. I tied the tarp to the trailer hitch and drove slowly to the burial ground. The pack began to filter out of the jungle and follow along beside me.

By this time, there were so many dead dogs, I had to dig trenches rather than individual holes. If I could, I laid the dogs that hung out together in life next to each other. Companions in life, companions in death, I thought. They deserved the honor in death that they never received in life.

After I'd buried these latest casualties, I did a head count. Several dogs were still missing.

I drove over to the metal storage containers to prep the food and get the dogs settled, then started to walk the area. Half the pack came with me. I walked through the boathouse and out the far side, stopping occasionally to whistle and listen for any dogs in the distance. Nothing.

I walked the paths through the jungle. I was the only person who came back here with the dogs.

I found footprints in a dried-up mud puddle and followed them until I arrived at what looked like an old campfire in a small clearing. There were bones and tufts of curly white fur among the charred bits of wood. I leaned in closer and moved the remains around with my machete. The dogs stood quietly by my side. There were two corpses, two dogs who had always been inseparable at the beach. I didn't want to disturb their bodies, so I decided to bury them there. I retrieved a five-gallon bucket from the truck and hauled sand from the beach back to the clearing to cover their bodies. The pack followed along, back and forth, until I was done. *Is this another dream? Why can't I wake up?* I couldn't keep my thoughts clear anymore.

It was harder than ever to leave the dogs that night.

When I got home, I showered, poured myself a tall glass of scotch, and went to sit by the pool to make the usual phone calls. I left a message on Melanie's voice mail, another on Nancy's. "Please, can we talk about how to get more dogs off the beach sooner rather than later?" I said. I was a little surprised to hear how shaky my voice was. "Please call me back." While Melanie and Nancy worked hard to find homes for Puerto Rico's strays, it was frustrating to watch the suffering of my dogs.

I needed to calm down. I was starting to feel light-headed, but it wasn't the scotch. I hadn't had enough to drink yet. I started to feel itchy and saw that I was breaking out in a rash. Was it the stress? The grass I sat in by the beach? Was the penicillin still in my system?

I stripped down and jumped in the pool. The cool water soothed my skin.

I finished my drink and went upstairs. I downed a couple of Benadryl and climbed into bed. Silently I begged my mind to take me to a happy place. I needed to escape the hell I was feeling. I curled into a ball and cried myself to sleep.

The next morning, Pam told me that I had talked and cried in my sleep all night long. I gave her the broad strokes of what had happened, but she could tell from my silence that it must have been bad.

Before she got out of the truck at her office, she turned to me and took my face in her hands. For the umpteenth time, she said: "I love you. And I don't want to lose you, Stephen. Please, be careful."

It broke my heart, and yet I was helpless to stop.

I had been at the beach for a couple of hours when I got a return call from Melanie.

"I just listened to your message. I'm so sorry! Are you okay?"

"Thanks, I'm all right." I didn't really feel like talking. I just wanted to be alone with my dogs.

"I'm going to talk to Nancy about doing another run down there."

"I'd be grateful, Melanie. Please make it happen. I'll contribute to the vet bills."

As it was, Pam and I were now spending between two and three thousand dollars a month on the dogs, depending on how many dogs were there at any given time. Since we'd first arrived seventeen months earlier, we'd increasingly given the dogs medical care at the beach, since island vets were disinclined to do so. Once we started sending the dogs to shelters stateside, we had no choice but to enlist professional veterinary help, which came in the form of Dr. Ramos in San Juan, the vet Nancy Guilford had taken some of the dogs to previously. However, the vet was expensive, so I continued to do as much as I could myself to keep the medical bills down while still making the dogs closer to ready for adoption—administering vaccinations and deworming, giving them medication, performing blood draws to check for heartworm, treating skin conditions. We'd also been chipping in to help pay for expenses after the dogs left the beach, once the rescue groups started taking some of them away. On average, it cost about $250 per dog for a checkup with Dr. Ramos and travel documents; this assumed we'd find a travel companion to fly the dog for free. On occasion, one of the dogs would have a serious complication that could add significantly to the cost.

Melanie sometimes muttered about how hard it was on her getting the dogs to the airport for shipment to shelters stateside. I usually let it slide, but I thought I should address the issue now.

"Melanie, I don't want to hear later that you're pissed off because you feel like you're doing all the work with the dogs once they leave the beach, okay?"

"What's that supposed to mean?" Clearly, she'd decided to get angry now rather than wait till later.

"I appreciate what you and Nancy do. I need your help down here. But I don't think you guys understand what I do with the dogs, you know?"

"I know you and Sandra feed and water the dogs every day, and I—"

"Are you serious?" I said, cutting her off. "That's what you think I do here seven days a week?"

"I know it's more than that. You're being sensitive. Let's talk about it later, okay?"

"It would be like me calling you a taxi driver for the dogs rather than a rescuer. You come to the beach, I put the dogs in the crates and load them in your vehicle. You drive them to the vet's office to be looked after. When they're healthy and ready to go, you transport them to the airport for someone else to take care of. This probably sounds a little insulting to you, doesn't it?"

"You know full well we do more than that! We're making calls—"

"I know you do more than that, but so do I. How do you think the dogs become such well-mannered, sweet animals?" I said, cutting her off again. I had never been so rude to her before, but I was tired of my work with the dogs being minimized. "I'm the guy training them and treating their health problems. I pay for the food and medical supplies. I comfort them when someone kills members of the pack. I bury the dead ones. So please show some respect for what I do." My voice was trembling with frustration.

"I'm sorry, Steve. It wasn't my intention to make you feel bad."

"As I see it, we're all an important part of the full picture. None of us could do this without the others."

The tension seemed to lift.

"I get it, Steve. I'll call you tomorrow after I speak with Nancy."

When I next spoke to Melanie, she had something other than a beach run on her agenda. Apparently she and Nancy and Martha had reached out to several people from various animal rights groups on the island about meeting with the mayor of Yabucoa and some of his people, as well as some of the local hotel owners, in hopes of coming up with a plan of action to make long-term changes for the stray dogs and other animals in the municipality.

Then she told me that one of the activists planning to attend the meeting was a manatee expert who wanted answers about the dead manatees that had washed up on shore. I found that odd, considering the fact that no one had done a damn thing about it back when I'd reported the occurrence weeks before. Evidently the bodies of the huge animals had taken a while to wash ashore; until then, the authorities and even the animal welfare groups had taken what I'd reported with a grain of salt. But it was hard for tourists to ignore a thousand-pound corpse peppered with crossbow arrows rotting on the beach.

"We felt that, in light of the television coverage and the hangings, a bit of outside pressure might motivate him to finally do something."

The idea was to present the mayor with the concept of using Yabucoa as a pilot program that could be an example for other communities.

"Given my experience with the mayor and his people, I'm skeptical." I had not forgotten the way the mayor's office had dismissed my complaint about the hotels' killing of the dogs. I had been back there a number of times since, always to be turned away.

"The mayor was apprehensive at first, but he finally agreed to hear what we have to say," Melanie told me.

"I guess it's progress that he agreed to sit down at all." I was open to putting a little more pressure on the officials, but I was nervous about what increased exposure might mean for the safety of my dogs.

"There's just one thing," Melanie said. "We think that, in light of your past interactions with the mayor and the police, your presence there might antagonize him."

"But shouldn't my voice be heard too? A bunch of people who have never even set foot on my beach speaking on behalf of my dogs and me? That's wrong and you know it!"

"I'm afraid that's all they'd hear, Steve," Melanie said.

She probably had a point, but it bothered me that I had to stay out of a meeting that could affect the problems I was facing daily. These other people only made guest appearances on the beach, but now they were taking control.

I talked with Pam about the meeting that night.

"Steve, you know how you get, especially about these dogs."

"Are you saying that I won't be able to hide my real feelings about the mayor?" I said, only half joking.

"Remember, it's about the dogs. If this meeting can help them, it's a good thing."

In the end, I agreed. I would feel even worse if I said something I regretted and the dogs paid the price.

"Why don't you come with me to Rhode Island next week?" Pam was traveling there on business. "It'll get you off the island just in case you have trouble resisting the urge to show up at that meeting."

"And I could hand-deliver my portfolio to RISD," I said. "Good idea." I had been hesitant to entrust my original artwork to the post office or UPS.

On the day of departure, the airport was busy, as always. After standing with our bags for a while, we finally snagged two seats in the waiting area by the gate. I'd put my artwork in an architectural drafting tube to protect it and slid the tube in the top of my backpack. I wasn't going to let it out of my sight.

While Pam went off to get us something to eat, I noticed a guy hovering nearby. I'd seen him earlier when we passed through security. I figured I was being paranoid, which wasn't surprising given what I'd experienced since arriving on the island.

When Pam returned with the sandwiches, I slid my pack to the ground next to my seat while we ate. When it was time to board, I grabbed my pack and off we went. On the plane, I stowed my bag in the overhead compartment and took my seat. Pam and I did our usual people-watching thing, waiting for the other passengers to stow their bags and get settled.

"My artwork! It's not here!" I had a flash of memory of putting my bag up top and realized the tube wasn't there. I jumped up and checked the compartment. "No! No! No!"

Pam saw the panic in my eyes. The flight attendant announced they were getting ready to shut the doors. I sat back down, defeated. All those hours and days of work to make my portfolio perfect, gone.

Pam wasn't ready to give up so easily. She called the flight attendant to our seats and explained the problem.

"I'm sorry, ma'am, but there's nothing we can do."

Another attendant overheard and came over. "Sit tight for a second," she said and walked toward the cockpit. A minute later, she returned down the aisle to our seats. "The captain agreed to hold the plane if you'd like to go back to the gate and look for your missing items."

I bolted out of my seat.

"Hurry! You have five minutes!" she called out after me.

I ran out of the plane and made a beeline for where we'd been sitting. There was nothing there. I ran back to security. Nothing there either. I felt sick. I returned to the plane and took my seat next to Pam. I said nothing, just pulled my sunglasses down over my eyes to hide my tears. I had no desire to be on this plane anymore, no reason to go to Rhode Island.

Pam wasn't giving up. She knew how much this meant to me. She got out of her seat and asked the flight attendant if she could go out and have a look around too. She did, but came back empty-handed.

"I'm sorry, sir, but we do have to shut the door and push back now," the flight attendant said.

"Could I have a strong drink?" I said.

The attendant smiled at me. "Of course, sweetie. I'm sorry you didn't find your package. Can it be replaced?"

Pam answered for me: "No."

I was speechless. I felt the plane push back. My drink arrived. I was about to down it and order another when I felt the plane stop, then move slowly back toward the gate. The staff opened the hatch. The airline employee who had helped me look around a few minutes earlier stepped on board. He was holding the tube!

Apparently he'd kept searching, checking all the garbage cans in the terminal. The last place he looked was the waste bin in the men's bathroom, and that's where he found my artwork.

Two days later, while the rescuers were meeting with the mayor in Yabucoa, I delivered my portfolio to the school. My relief was boundless.

That evening, Melanie and Nancy called. It sounded like they had been celebrating.

"The mayor came through! He's giving us a thousand dollars toward a shelter for the dogs."

"Wow, really?" I was amazed and excited.

"He also promised that he'd call one of us if there were any problems with the dogs at the beach instead of hiring some outside agency to euthanize them."

I was stunned.

"His only condition was that the shelter be located in Yabucoa."

I hung up full of hope that this was the beginning of something really wonderful.

As soon as we got back to Puerto Rico, I began looking for a place we could set up as a shelter in the area. I spent hours each day looking around the local communities with a real estate agent for a rental home with property that would accommodate a shelter. I harbored hope that Sandra and her husband, Angel, would live there and act as caregivers to the dogs. They had both been unemployed since I'd met them, each living with his or her respective parents. Pam and I thought this would be a great way for them to live together as an independent couple again.

None of the properties exactly fit the bill, but a few were close, and we made offers, hoping that with a little creativity we could make it work. The agent was friends with some of the owners and assured us that they were animal lovers—a few of the properties had previously kept horses, and we thought we could convert the old stables to kennels—but the deals kept falling apart with no explanation. "The owner changed his mind," the agent said.

On top of that, Sandra and Angel weren't that thrilled with the idea when we presented it to them. I think they were concerned about attracting attention to themselves from the people who hated the work we were doing with the dogs at the beach—they were always asking me to keep quiet, like so many others had. And to be fair, they would have been left alone caring full time for the dogs in the middle of the jungle. It wasn't that appealing an offer.

So even if we found the perfect location, we couldn't have a shelter without caretakers.

One afternoon, Martha called from Florida to weigh in. She hadn't been around much lately, but Melanie and Nancy had been keeping her in the loop.

"Maybe you and Pam could live at the shelter."

"We have a contract on our house, Martha, we can't just pick up and move. And before you say anything, I don't see any of you volunteering to relocate either."

While the shelter effort stalled, things continued to go downhill at the beach. In March I came upon a bunch of guys dragging a horse behind a pickup truck. I was still some distance away when I saw the horse fall down and try frantically to get up, kicking the pickup a few times in the process. It appeared the men inside were not amused. They got out with baseball bats and proceeded to beat her until she stopped struggling, tied her feet together with rope, and resumed dragging her. When they saw me, one of the men got out and cut her loose. The truck took off.

I got out and walked slowly over to her. She was still alive, but barely. Her skin had come off from where she'd made contact with the road. She tried to raise her head to sniff me. I petted her face and talked gently to her until she died. And then I fell apart.

A horse was too big for me to move or bury. I thought about burning her right there, but in the end left her corpse to rot, knowing that its stench might keep the thugs who killed my dogs away. But when the corpse was still there after several days, I couldn't sit by anymore. It was time for another visit to the mayor's office.

I spoke to the receptionist at the front desk and asked to see the mayor.

"He is not here."

I explained the reason for my visit.

"I can send someone down to the beach to speak with you later today."

They wouldn't talk to me here, but they'd go out of their way to come to the beach? That didn't make any sense. Until it did.

The mayor's assistant, Jose Abril, showed up with a couple of other guys later that day. He was a smart dresser and spoke great English. I was hopeful he'd be sympathetic.

But it quickly became obvious that he was just pretending to care. As he prattled on with small talk, I had a feeling he'd made the trip to put a pacifier in my mouth. I was having trouble being polite.

"I appreciate you coming all the way out here, but what I really want is for the mayor to do something about the constant slaughter of my dogs. And these other mutilated animals are turning up now—the manatees, the horse. He's got to find out who's behind all of this."

Jose took a step toward me and put a hand on my shoulder. His smile disappeared. "Steve, you seem like a nice guy. But you need to stop coming to the beach and talking to the media. Do I make myself clear?"

In the calmest voice I could muster, I said, "Jose, take your hand off my shoulder unless you want to lose it."

He removed his hand, but he wasn't backing down. "You're making a mistake. I don't think you understand me."

His two cronies stepped forward.

I put my hand on my hip and pulled open the Velcro flap that held the Taser to my belt. "Back the fuck up. You may think you're intimidating, but you're not."

Jose maintained eye contact with me but put his hand up. The men stopped.

"Look, Steve, I'm about your only friend here," he said.

I laughed, which seemed to surprise him.

"You have managed to piss off a lot of people in powerful positions. If you don't stop, they'll shut you up."

"Jose, did you just threaten me?"

"Walk away, Steve, and don't look back. Don't talk to people. Just enjoy the island and all of its beauty."

"You've got to be kidding me," I said, laughing at the outrageousness of what he'd just said.

Even though my brain was begging me to be reasonable, I couldn't shut up. "Jose, again I ask, are you threatening me?"

"Steve, I think we're on the same page here," he said, skirting the question. I guess he thought I would simply comply with his request.

"You guys must feel so tough. But you're all a bunch of pussies. Three against one? Oh boy!"

Feeling threatened, I reached for my Taser again, but the thought of rotting in a Puerto Rican jail for frying the mayor's assistant stopped me. I turned and walked away before I changed my mind.

Moments later, sitting in my truck, trying to fit the key in the ignition, I realized how badly I was shaking. My instincts told me this wasn't over, not by a long shot.

THIRTY-THREE

I stewed over Jose Abril's threats for several days. I wanted to get the media involved; someone needed to tell the world what had happened to the horse. I tried to reach Susan Saltaro at Univision, without success. Other media outlets told me they already knew who I was, and that I wasn't news. Finally, I managed to contact someone at Channel 4 news in San Juan, who agreed to send a reporter to the beach the following morning.

The woman who showed up was dressed to the nines—six-inch heels and a miniskirt that left little to the imagination. She was beautiful. I'm sure she had a loyal viewership. But she spoke nearly no English, and she was clearly uncomfortable with fifty or more dogs sniffing at her legs and jamming their noses up her skirt. She and the cameraman were both disturbed by the sight of the decomposing horse, its legs still tied. It was brutal, but I wanted them to see that I wasn't making up the story.

Fortunately, the cameraman spoke pretty good English and offered to be our interpreter. In the end, the interview went pretty well. I told her, with his help, about the horse, and the story aired that evening.

The following morning, more than a dozen dogs were missing. I grabbed my weapons from the truck and raced along the path. There they were: garbage bags.

A few days later, Martha called. "Hey, Steve. Sandra told me about the horse, so I called the mayor's office. I need you to go meet with a guy named Jose."

"Hell, no!"

"Can I ask why?"

"I don't want to talk about it."

"Steve, the mayor is really angry with you for going to the media. He's insisting you apologize."

"He can kiss my ass, Martha."

"You should have gone to him first, Steve. Let him handle it."

"Hey, Martha? When you talked to Jose, did he happen to tell you that we already met about the horse?"

She said nothing.

"I didn't think so. I asked for their help. Jose threatened me, Martha. I called the media because he did nothing to help. I had to bury a dozen of my dogs the day after the story ran."

"I'm sorry, Steve. I know it's hard. But you need to look at the big picture—"

"How many dogs have *you* buried, Martha?"

She started to cry. I didn't care.

"Forget the mayor and his apology."

That evening when I got home, I e-mailed Martha photos I'd taken of the horse and the mutilated dogs in garbage bags.

In the morning, I swung by the mayor's office. The receptionist at the front desk looked nervous when I walked in. She recognized me. Before I said anything, she said, "His Honor isn't in the office today. Would you like to leave a message?"

I saw Jose in the back hallway, close enough to hear what I was saying.

"Yes, actually, I would. Please tell the mayor, 'Fuck you. You don't scare me.'"

I turned and walked away. My knees nearly buckled from fear. I wondered if I'd be arrested for threatening a public official.

Martha called that afternoon in tears. She'd looked at the photos I'd sent.

"I had no idea, Steve." It was hard to make out what she was saying between sobs. "Melanie and I are really worried you're going to turn up missing one of these days."

"I am too, Martha."

"But we have an idea that might help. The next time you find dead dogs, take more pictures like the ones you sent me, and get tissue samples. We'll hire a forensic specialist to find out how the dogs died."

"It's obvious how the dogs died, Martha. Their heads were cut off."

One morning I came across one of the young mothers wandering around looking lost. For several weeks, I'd seen her with her litter where she kept them hidden safely in the jungle. My first thought was that someone had found her pups and taken them.

The little mother followed me around whimpering. Even when I held her in my arms, she wouldn't stop. Her teats were engorged with milk. She needed her puppies to nurse. It was going to be extremely painful for her until her milk dried up.

I called Sandra to see if she knew anything about the missing pups. There was no answer, so I left her a message. A couple of days passed without a word. I called again and left another message.

I finally ran into Sandra at the beach.

"I'm so sorry I didn't call you back," she said.

When I asked her about the puppies, she looked away sheepishly.

"Sandra?"

"I was worried about them, so I called Martha about them last week. I was afraid they wouldn't make it."

"Did you take the puppies to send to Martha?"

"She said she would keep them until they were ready to be adopted."

"They were three weeks old, Sandra, too young to be separated from their mother. She was taking care of them."

Sandra was quiet.

"Where are they now?"

"I think Martha flew them to Florida a couple of days ago."

I turned away to retrieve the food from the back of the truck. The little mother dog was at my feet still whimpering. I picked her up and she nuzzled my neck.

I wanted to call Martha and chew her out for acting without thinking things through. Her heart was in the right place, but she didn't ask the right questions. Sandra would say anything to get the dogs off the beach.

After settling the dogs down with their morning meal, I broke down and dialed Martha's office number. As expected, the secretary answered.

"Who may I say is calling?"

I hesitated for a moment. "Sandra Cintron," I said.

"I'll transfer you immediately."

While I was on hold, I wondered what the secretary must have thought about my deep voice.

"Hey, Sandra!" Martha said when she came on the line. "How are you?"

"I'm good, Martha. Thanks for asking."

There was silence on the other end of the line.

"Do you have a minute?"

"Sure, Steve. What's up?" The bubbly tone that had been there a minute ago had disappeared. In truth, I think we were all getting a little sick of each other.

"I know how hard you're working to help the dogs, and I really appreciate it."

"I'm doing the best I can."

"The puppies you had Sandra send you last week? Do you know how old they were?"

"I was worried they wouldn't make it, Steve. I had to do something."

"They were in a safe area," I said. "They had a great mother taking care of them."

"I can find homes for puppies easier than I can for adult dogs. You know that is true."

"But they were too young, Martha! And the mum is under ten pounds—she'd be an easy placement."

"I didn't know she was so small."

"She's in a lot of pain, Martha. She needed to nurse those pups."

Martha started to cry.

"I didn't call to upset you. I just want you to understand that I know these dogs better than anyone, than you, than Melanie, than Nancy. You are all awesome, but please talk to me before you take the dogs. I'll tell you the truth—those puppies should have gone with their mother. It shouldn't have happened like this. It can't happen again."

"Fair enough," she said.

"Thanks for listening, Martha. Call me if you need me."

Soon after that, Pam and I were invited to a party at Nancy Guilford's house in San Juan. I wasn't terribly keen on going at first, but then I thought it might be a good opportunity to spend time with the others in a more relaxed setting, away from the horrors at the beach. Pam and I both thought it would be good to unwind and have a laugh for a change.

We were greeted at the door with open arms, handed mojitos, and invited in to join the party. I didn't know most of the people there, but Nancy took us around to introduce us to the other guests. Apparently Nancy and Melanie had told people what Pam and I were doing in Yabucoa.

We got to talking to a couple of older ladies named Patty and Eleanor who asked lots of questions. "If you need anything, please don't hesitate to call us."

Thinking I must have missed something, I asked, "How do you know Nancy?"

They chuckled. "We used to do rescue like you. We were the original founders of the oldest dog rescue group on the island. Now we're too old, but we still do what we can."

"It's an honor to meet you!" I said, truly relieved to meet like-minded people. "Thank you for pioneering the way." I gave them both a hug.

They looked at Pam and said, "Honey, he's a keeper!"

Pam looked at me and smiled. "Yes, he is."

As the night wore on and the drinks flowed, Nancy got a little maudlin about the dogs. On her computer, she pulled up some of the photos I'd taken and started to cry. "I would have saved them!" Everyone was looking at her, slack-jawed.

I leaned over to Pam and whispered, "Let's get out of here." I noticed that a few other people had the same idea and were edging toward the door.

Before we could make our escape, a young woman grabbed my arm. "Excuse me? Can I come see Dead Dog Beach with you sometime?"

She caught me a little off guard. "Sure, whenever. I'm there every day."

One of the older ladies came over with a smile on her face. "Steve, this is Anna. She's come from Boston and she's staying with me for a few days. She's been wanting to do some rescue work since she got here. I think you're just the guy to show her what it's all about."

I was pretty flattered, considering the source of the recommendation. Patty gave me her home number and said to call her. We made arrangements for me to pick Anna up in the morning.

I said to Anna, "I hope you're an early riser!"

The following morning, I arrived at Patty's house to find Anna in sweats. I laughed. "You might want to wear lighter clothing."

She changed into something more suitable for the climate and we were on our way. During the drive, I told her about all the dogs and some of my experiences over the past eighteen months.

"Oh my gawd! You're amazing!" She sounded like Fran Drescher. I'm sure she thought she'd embarrassed me from the look on my face. "No, really, what you're doing with the dogs is amazing." Yep, she sounded just like a Boston version of Fran Drescher.

The dogs were there to greet us, just like I'd promised. Anna started in with the same high-pitched baby voice that everyone who visited the beach the first time seemed to use with the dogs. I had to put the brakes on that right away.

"Can you please talk normally to them?" I hated to embarrass her, but I didn't want the dogs getting overexcited and jumping all over her.

"Why? They're dogs, not humans."

"Trust me, you'll get more from the experience if you follow my lead."

I walked around with her, introducing her to the dogs and describing the layout of the beach. She started to relax, and the more she did, the more the dogs warmed up to her.

I noticed that the young mother whose pups Sandra had taken prematurely wasn't around. I knew she was depressed and starting to isolate herself from the pack. This wasn't good.

I took Anna to the spot in the jungle where the dog had made her den, and sure enough there she was, her little face peeking out of the foliage as we walked up. Anna melted on the spot. When I called to her, the little dog trotted over, her head down and her tail between her legs. I picked her up and chanted my little mantra to her: "Shush . . . shush . . . shush . . . shush . . . it's okay . . . it's okay . . . it's okay." In no time, she was a puddle in my arms. Anna had tears rolling down her face. I placed the little dog in Anna's arms. I could tell it was a happily-ever-after moment. It was like they were made for each other.

"I can't believe they took her puppies!" Anna said. As she held that little dog, her fury over the injustice grew. "What the hell were those people thinking?"

I realized at that moment that I wouldn't want to cross this chick. She was pretty tough. I'd rather have her as a wingman than an enemy.

We finished doing rounds with the dogs around noon. Anna was anxious to get back to San Juan to have the little dog checked out by a vet. It looked like Anna was taking someone back with her to Boston.

I couldn't have been happier.

THIRTY-FOUR

I found the second horse, drawn and quartered by pickup trucks, a tiny puppy curled up inside the bloody carcass for warmth. Later I found the rest of the litter nursing on the poisoned corpse of their mother. The puppies were sweet and playful, but it was obvious they weren't healthy.

I got some shampoo from the truck and took the pups to the shallow water along the shore to give them a proper bath. The water was warm, so it wouldn't be too much of a shock to their delicate little systems. They needed to be cleaned up and disinfected. Afterward, I sat in the back of the truck with the hatch open, cuddling them in a towel to warm them up while I made some phone calls. I left messages with Melanie, Nancy, and Martha. For once their fixation on puppies could be a help here. I tried to nurse the little guys from baby bottles filled with artificial mother's milk, but they weren't interested. At least they enjoyed the canned puppy food I put down for them. I made a little nest for them in an empty room in the boathouse, separate from the main puppy room so the other puppies wouldn't get sick.

The following afternoon, Martha called me.

"Sandra found the new puppies this morning," she told me. "How could you isolate them like that? It's cruel, Steve."

"Martha, they had to be quarantined. They could have parvo or distemper. We need to get them checked out and treated before putting the other puppies at risk."

It was too late. Sandra had already put the sick puppies in with the others.

Over the next few days, I noticed that some of the other puppies were starting to show signs of illness. And then one morning, I discovered all the puppies were gone. I called Sandra.

"Angel and I took them to San Juan so they can go to shelters in the States." This was the first time they hadn't checked with me first in a while.

I was furious, but not because they had taken the dogs without my okay. In any other circumstance, I'd have been thrilled that the dogs were on their way to potential homes. But if the puppies were sick and sent to a shelter in the States, the entire project could be compromised.

That Saturday I took two cases of bleach to disinfect the puppy room. Eight gallons of toxic cleaner and six hours later, Sandra and I had nearly suffocated cleaning the place up.

For days I waited for word about the puppies they had taken, but nothing. I knew something was wrong. I could feel it. A week later, I heard through the grapevine that some of the puppies they had sent to a shelter in the Northeast had arrived very sick. They were severely dehydrated from vomiting and diarrhea. They died shortly thereafter. Apparently the same thing happened to another rescuer who had taken some of the puppies in until they got flights off the island. The sick puppies nearly wiped out all the healthy rescue pups she had in her home.

I had buried more than a thousand dogs. I had named each of them, fed and nurtured and cared for every single one. I had given them time, food, medicine, and love. With a lot of hard work, I'd managed to turn them back into healthy dogs. I'd socialized them and taught them tricks so that if they ever had the opportunity to move to a real home, they'd be ready. Instead, they were forever consigned to the burial ground at the beach.

Melanie Shapiro and Nancy Guilford heard from a contact of theirs high up the chain of command in the San Juan Police Department that I was being targeted by just about everyone with a vested interest in cleaning up the beach. They were killing my dogs to intimidate me—hanging, poisoning, decapitating, dismembering, torching—nothing was beyond them. They knew my routines and where I walked on the beach.

Everybody I spoke to suggested I stop going to the beach—neighbors, acquaintances, Pam's coworkers.

And I was finally near the breaking point. For the past few months I had started limiting my wandering around the beach to an area close enough to my truck to make a quick getaway. I had become paranoid about every vehicle that passed or was parked in the near distance. I knew I was being watched. If I approached a vehicle, it quickly sped away. Where once I had left my weapons in my truck, now I carried them with me at all times. I'd practiced reaching for them so many times, I knew exactly how quickly I could access the machete or Taser.

One morning a couple of fishermen and their wives came to talk to me. They'd just seen me carrying a couple of dead dogs across the parking lot to the burial ground.

"We've seen what you do here for a long time now. People here talk about you. They say you are a hated man."

I had pissed off too many people by going to the media and exposing the problems at the beach. How sad was it that people wanted to kill me because I fed dogs? But I realized it went deeper than that. What I was doing was interfering with their pocketbooks, and making their culture look bad.

But I wasn't ready to stop. Another morning, another day at the beach. I spotted several of my dogs lying on their sides on the gravel in the middle of the parking lot. Occasionally the dogs would sun themselves, but this was different. They didn't move when I drove closer. The rest of the pack filtered out of the jungle slowly, walking in front of the truck so that I had to be careful not to bump them.

When I parked and got out, I surveyed the area but I didn't see anything out of the ordinary. A couple of the dogs had tried to get in the truck when I opened the door, as though they were trying to get away from something. I scoured the perimeter of the parking lot, then over toward the boathouse and up to the conveyer belt that ran along the top several stories up. My senses were tingling. I wanted to make sure the path was clear before I went to the dead dogs.

I unhooked my machete and walked to where they lay. The pack was acting twitchy and nervous. A few scattered and headed back to the jungle. The pack wasn't the same as it had been. We'd lost so many of the leaders. There were a lot of newcomers now, young and unfamiliar with the threats at the beach. Only a few of them stood with confidence at my side.

I got to the first dog and knelt at her side. I looked her over to see any sign that she'd been hit by a car, but there was nothing to indicate that. Her body was intact and warm to the touch. But she was lying in a pool of blood. Where was it coming from? I lifted her head and found a small hole in her neck. It looked like a bullet hole. I slid my hand under her neck and found a much larger wound: an exit wound.

I quickly went to the other dogs to see if the same was true for them. They had all been shot.

I felt a wave of panic. What if the killers were still around? I scanned the area again but saw no movement, heard no sound.

My instincts were telling me to leave, but I couldn't leave without burying them. They would be flattened by someone driving across the lot if I didn't take care of it now.

I slid my hands under the first dog and lifted her. She was still floppy. She hadn't been dead long.

I looked around as I carried her across the lot to the truck, her face up against my left ear. I had one hand under her shoulder and the other under her bottom. I was still holding her when I heard the whiz and whoosh of another bullet hitting her body. Her body twitched from the impact; blood sprayed across my shoulder.

The dogs scattered. I dropped the body and ran for cover behind the metal storage containers. I couldn't tell where the shooting was coming from. I was afraid to look. My knees wobbled beneath me as I leaned against the container. I could feel my heart beating in my head. The driver's-side door of my truck was still open. I fumbled with the keys in my pocket, almost dropping them. My chest hurt. I looked to see if I'd been hit, but it was only the dog's blood. I took a deep breath and made a break for it, but I slipped in the gravel as I rounded the containers and fell on my side. I jumped right back up and was behind the wheel in a few short steps. I jammed the key in the ignition and fired up the engine, pulling a fast U-turn.

The next thing I knew, I was at an intersection a couple of miles up the road. *If I turn right, I go home. If I go straight, I go to the police station.* I didn't trust anyone anymore. I went home.

A few weeks later, Nancy Guilford moved back to Florida.

THIRTY-FIVE

My application to RISD was accepted. I was elated. Until then, Pam and I had been seriously considering renewing her contract to stay in Puerto Rico for two more years. We both still harbored a dream of living a normal life there, in the paradise we'd imagined when we first arrived. I also couldn't bear the thought of never seeing my dogs again. And we really had nowhere else to go. But once the letter arrived, we changed plans. We quickly purchased another old farmhouse in Rhode Island with an eye toward fixing it up while I was in school.

I needed to make an appearance at the school to finalize a few things with my undergraduate credits, so Pam and I decided to make the trip back to Rhode Island with a few dogs that we wanted to get into stateside shelters. We made arrangements for a night flight into Newark Airport. This would mean traveling during the coolest part of the day in the shortest amount of time, which meant less stress on the animals. From New Jersey, we'd rent a vehicle large enough to transport them the rest of the way.

Hurricane season is not to be taken lightly when you live in the tropics, so we made extra preparations to batten down the house while we were away, just in case a storm blew through during the week we were gone. I closed and locked the hurricane shutters on every window and door. I closed and locked the garage just before we drove to the airport.

Funnily enough, it felt good to be back in Rhode Island. Everything looked brighter and felt a lot more peaceful after all the hair-raising experiences we'd been through in Puerto Rico. It was beautiful there. We dropped in to see a few of our friends. It was really lovely, and the week flew by.

Pam needed to get back to Puerto Rico for work, but I wanted to hang around a few more days getting the animals situated. I dropped her at the airport on Sunday and went back to the big empty house that would be our home in a few months. I was outside cutting the grass when Pam called to let me know she had arrived safely in San Juan.

"Call me when you get back to the house, okay?" I said before we hung up.

The drone of the lawn mower must have drowned out my ringtone when she checked in later, and I missed her call. When I listened to her message, my heart skipped a beat. Then it skipped a few more.

I couldn't make out everything she said, but through the screaming and crying I heard "robbed" and "broken in" and "smashed."

I tried to call her back but it went straight to her voice mail.

I called again. Same thing.

On the third try, she answered. "I'm standing in the living room. They stole everything!"

There was a heavy lock on the steel cage over our front door (a regular feature of homes down there), which was intact. But inside, there was chaos. Pam—a veteran of years of California's finest seismic activity, thought there'd been an earthquake. The TV cabinet was tipped over, everything was out of drawers and on the floor. But things got weird in the kitchen. There were ice cream containers on the counter, the fridge was open, all the food inside spoiling. And then she saw the back door swinging in the wind, one of the panes of glass broken inward and the lock drilled out.

What she said next was a little muffled, as though she'd moved her mouth away from the phone: "You better get the hell out of here!"

"Pam, who are you shouting at?"

"I don't know if they're still here!"

"Pam, get out of the house right now! Get in the truck and drive to a public place."

I could hear her breathing hard as she ran. I was relieved when I heard the beep of the alarm on the truck indicating that she was getting in. I heard the door shut and the engine turn over.

"Lock the door!" I screamed.

"I'm driving away from the house now." She sounded calmer, but only marginally.

"Just keep driving around the compound until we can get in touch with one of the other expats. Hang tight. I'll call you right back."

I hung up and dialed her supervisor, Bryan, but it went to his voice mail. I was reluctant to leave a message, but I left one anyway. Luckily, he called back immediately.

"I'm calling Pam's cell right now," he said. "Let me see what I can do."

I waited impatiently for Bryan or Pam or anyone to call me back and tell me what was going on. I wanted to hear that Pam was safe.

While I was cooling my heels in Rhode Island, Pam had managed to reach her coworker Pablo. The three of them met at the Palmas del Mar front gate and went to the house together, where they waited for the security company to arrive. Bryan and Pablo had no idea how bad it was until they went inside and saw for themselves what had happened. The back door had been tampered with and the windows next to the door handle were busted out. It appeared the burglars had drilled and disassembled the lock to get in. The door didn't shut properly and would need a new handle before anyone could safely stay in the house. Bryan insisted Pam stay with him until I returned.

"Bryan's working on a flight back for you," she told me later when we spoke. I felt better knowing that her friends were looking after her, but it bothered me that I wasn't there for her. I spent the next forty-eight hours finding a place for the dogs. A woman named Osa, a real animal lover, volunteered to take them while I was back in Puerto Rico.

I got an early plane heading south, trying to come to terms with all our personal possessions having been stolen or destroyed. This was not how I wanted to leave the island. But the thing weighing heaviest on my mind was the dogs, of course. What was going to happen to them? Who would take care of them now? Sandra had little to no money to spend on food and visited the dogs only when she could afford to feed them.

Bryan picked me up at the airport.

"Pam's hanging in there," he said. "Don't worry about a thing. We're here to help."

"I really appreciate it, man."

The drive to the compound seemed awfully long. I'm usually very chatty, but I was quiet, thinking about the mess that awaited me.

I felt my heartbeat quicken as we drove up the hill right before our house.

Bryan looked over at me. "You okay?"

"Yeah, I'm fine."

"I've made arrangements for packers and a moving truck to get you guys out of here. They start tomorrow."

I sat quietly. This was all happening so fast.

Pam burst into tears when I walked in the front door. I was speechless. It looked like a bomb had gone off in the middle of our living room. Pam's friend Karina, a Puerto Rican native whom she knew from work, was helping Pam clean out the rotten food in the refrigerator. Karina had also been extremely helpful to Pam in dealing with the local police during the investigation.

It appeared that the burglars had made themselves at home. They'd not only stolen or destroyed everything of value, they'd left remnants of the food and booze they'd helped themselves to on the kitchen table.

"I want to come see the house right away," our landlady, Blanca, called to say.

"Could you wait until tomorrow? It's not a good time right now," I said.

She started to scream at me.

"Settle down!" I was in no mood for this bullshit. "You need to talk to the real estate agent and make arrangements with her to enter the premises."

"I don't want to talk to you. I want Pam."

She hung up the phone and within seconds Pam's cell phone rang. Pam looked at me and shrugged. She took the call. After a few minutes, she hung up.

"She's coming by to see the damage tomorrow. She wanted to bring Berto, but I said absolutely not."

Berto was the handyman I'd fired several months earlier for entering the house without our permission. I had just gotten out of the upstairs shower one day when I heard someone downstairs in the living room. I was halfway downstairs when I saw him with a beer in his hand.

"What are you doing here?"

He choked on a mouthful of beer. "I thought no one was home."

"And that would make it okay for you to be in my house?"

He looked angry. "Blanca owns this house, not you! She employs me to take care of this place."

I felt a little vulnerable dressed only in a towel, but I wasn't backing down. "I have a contract stating that she needs to give me forty-eight hours notice—in writing—if she wants to enter the house. So get out before I call the police!"

He mouthed *"Fuck you"* as he turned and stormed out.

I called Blanca to complain, and she said, "There's nothing I can do."

Furious, I called the real estate agent and asked to have someone change the locks. I sent Blanca the bill. I'd been on her shit list ever since. I didn't care—I wasn't letting Berto in my house.

"He showed up with the security guard when Bryan and Pablo and I first got here," Pam said. "I didn't let him in."

The next day, while the movers were busy shoveling the remains of our damaged possessions into boxes, Blanca called Pam from the end of the driveway. Pam went out to speak to her.

"This is going to come out of your security deposit," I overheard Blanca say. I kept my distance, knowing that I would say something I'd regret. In a little while, Pam and Blanca went to the real estate agent's office to take care of the paperwork. I knew it wasn't going to go well, but there was nothing I could do, so I decided to focus on finishing up at the house.

I went to the backyard to clean the bits of leaves and grass clippings out of the pool. The movers were still inside, working toward having the truck packed by the end of the day. I needed to be by myself for a little while. I was upset about the way things had happened. We had come here with such open hearts and minds, ready and willing to embrace anything the new culture could throw our way. Instead, our dreams of living a fantasy life on a tropical Caribbean island had been dashed. Was I supposed to learn something from this? I was angry that the next day would be our last in Puerto Rico. We still needed to go to the police station to get the final report for the insurance company. I felt a pain in my heart when the next thought came to me: the dogs. I had to say good-bye to them. I felt sick at the thought. I flirted with the idea of skipping it. They'd never know the difference, right? I couldn't do that. I owed them at least a good-bye.

As these thoughts swirled through my brain, I caught a movement along the top of the garden wall. *Probably an iguana.* Then I got the distinct feeling that I was being watched. I looked up and squinted. A man in his early twenties was squatting on his heels atop the wall. Between us were the pool and a chest-high concrete shed that covered the pool pump. I stood there for a moment wondering if I was really seeing him or if I'd truly lost it and was seeing things. He wore a sweat-stained wifebeater and baggy pants with boots. A snide little grin came over his face. He started to laugh. He raised both hands and flipped me a double bird.

Something inside me snapped.

In one leap, I hopped across the six-foot-wide section of the pool, rounded the corner, and in one Jackie Chan–like move I was on top of the pump house and running down the top of the wall. The edge was about eight inches wide. The yard had a steep slope, and I was getting farther off the ground the farther I chased him. I think I caught him off guard by how quickly I went after him. I had almost reached him when he jumped off the wall and into the jungle on the other side of the property.

I saw red. I wanted to beat the little bastard within an inch of his life. I wanted retribution.

A voice in the back of my mind was screaming at me to stop. I ignored it.

In my peripheral vision, I saw movement in the tall grass. I wobbled to a halt, nearly losing my footing. When I looked again, I saw a dozen men waiting below with machetes. A wave of vertigo overtook me as I looked down at them, about twelve feet below where I stood.

They started to taunt me. The young man I'd chased was in the middle of the pack, laughing his ass off.

I hated them all. I wanted to make them pay. I scanned their faces.

I wrestled with humility and mortality. If I didn't walk away, I'd likely die fighting. It was what they'd wanted all along.

I walked the walk of shame back along the top of the wall while they called out to me in Spanish. I didn't understand the words, but I knew they were mocking me.

I looked back toward the house to see the moving men walking along the wall toward me.

"Are you okay?" the lead man asked.

"Be careful. There's a bunch of guys back there that tried to jump me."

The movers called out to my attackers in Spanish, warning them to leave. The posse yelled back, but slowly their voices faded into the jungle.

I called Pam, who was still at the real estate agent's office.

"Stay in the house with the movers, Steve. Please."

When Pam returned a few hours later, she told me that Blanca finally understood the seriousness of the situation when Pam told her what had just happened to me. We weren't just bailing on the house; Pam's company was sending us home for safety reasons. But it was Wednesday afternoon and we were scheduled to leave on Friday. Blanca had us over a barrel. She charged us the next two months' rent and kept the security deposit. We had no leverage to fight her. Still, the money she squeezed us for was a fraction of what we lost in the robbery.

The following day we went to get the official police report. Although I was all too familiar with the station in Yabucoa, I'd never been to the station in Humacao. After a day of jumping through hoops and being shuttled from one clerk to another, we finally sat down with the detective on the case.

"There have been several break-ins in the community lately. We're looking into several suspects."

"The way your house was ransacked, it might have been someone who knew you'd be away."

"Steve, here's another thing to consider," the detective said, leaning toward me, his elbows on the desk. "You're pretty well known around here, you know what I mean?"

I smiled. "How so?"

He smiled back. "I think what you've done with the dogs is great. But you have made enemies. There are people who feel you have made them look bad, people who can hurt you. Or worse. Steve, you can't beat them. It'll end badly for you and your family. Please listen to me. I'm on your side."

"Thanks, man. It's nice to know there are still a few good cops around."

"Yeah, there are a few of us," he said with a chuckle. "Now go home and be safe, okay?"

I reached out to shake his hand as I stood up to leave.

"What you have done for the dogs means a lot for all of us who care about animals," he said. "Thank you."

I had tears in my eyes hearing him say that.

He escorted us to the exit.

"Thanks again, bro," I said.

"My pleasure, my friend. You take care of yourself and your beautiful wife."

THIRTY-SIX

I had a feeling that saying good-bye to my dogs was going to be the hardest thing I'd ever done, and I'd been through some things I didn't think I'd survive.

A few hours before we were due to fly out, I pulled up to the beach for the last time. The dogs came out to greet me like always, following alongside the truck, happy to see me. I'd been crying since I left Bryan's house a half hour earlier. The dogs could sense something was wrong. The nudged at me and whined. Even the dogs that were usually more standoffish were vying for attention.

I tried to go about my normal routine. I set out food and water. But instead of the other chores I usually performed, I sat down in the middle of the pack while they ate. Dogs licked and nudged me. A few crawled into my lap.

I started to sob. I felt the way I did when I had buried my friends day after day. Twelve hundred of them, in the end.

The dogs knew their alpha was hurting. They didn't understand why, of course, but they sensed that I needed them at my side, and they were there.

I hated leaving them behind. I didn't even know if I could. I looked at every dog, taking a mental photograph of each one. I promised myself that I would never forget them or what they had done for me. I was lost when I had found them that day at the beach. Life had lost the vibrancy it held when I was younger. What had happened to my idealistic dreams? When did I give up? Meeting the dogs had given me purpose. I felt alive when I was with them. And now I was abandoning them.

I always lost track of time when I was with my pack, so I had set the alarm on my watch before I left the house. I felt my heart lurch when the watch started to beep.

"Not yet!" I cried.

I felt the dogs' noses against my skin as they nuzzled me, sending a shiver through my body. I cried harder than I had in years, and I had cried a lot in the two years we'd been in Puerto Rico.

"I'm sorry, you guys." The dogs looked me in the eyes as though trying to understand what I was saying. Their heads tilted and their brows furrowed. They looked so sad.

"I'm sorry for leaving you."

I felt like I had a thousand pounds on my back as I walked to the truck. I climbed in and pulled the door shut behind me. I had to blink away the tears so I could see the road. The dogs followed as I slowly drove out of the parking lot. I couldn't bear it. I punched the accelerator and sped away. I looked in the rearview mirror and saw the entire pack standing on the road watching me leave. It felt like my heart was being ripped from my chest.

When I rounded the corner and was out of sight of the dogs, I pulled over, opened the door, and threw up. I sat there for several minutes, trying to catch my breath. I knew I'd never recover from this.

B ack in Rhode Island, I descended into a dark, lonely place to grieve. I felt like I'd died inside.

    Despite my state of mind, I started at the Rhode Island School of Design that September, and began work on restoring our farmhouse. Built in 1862, the house had a ton of character but all manner of structural problems that needed my attention. I completely tuned out everything happening in Puerto Rico.

And then, on the morning of my birthday in October, I received a desperate e-mail from a rescuer, begging me for help. I knew my departure would result in renewed attacks on the dogs, but I didn't know how bad it would get.

The city of Barceloneta had put together an ordinance prohibiting the ownership of animals in all public housing projects. It stated that "animals represent a grave aesthetic and health problem to the city of Barceloneta." The ordinance did not specify which animals were okay; it simply forbade them all. So in early October, with the blessings of the mayor, a private animal control firm went door-to-door, violently confiscating some eighty healthy cats and dogs, ostensibly to relocate them to a nearby shelter.

The truth came out later that day. Instead of being moved to a shelter, the pets had been thrown to their deaths from a fifty-foot-high freeway bridge nearby. Miraculously, six had managed to survive the fall.

An Associated Press investigation discovered that these inhumane killings were far more widespread than the one incident. Their investigation revealed a scale of viciousness far beyond what most rescuers had suspected.

A former employee of one of the animal control companies had told the AP that over the years, thousands of pets had been rounded up and brutally killed, their bodies dumped. He'd even led the AP to two killing fields, where rotting corpses and bones were found.

The investigation started a firestorm of public protest nationally and internationally, as well as a rash of lawsuits.

Eighty pets had made the ultimate sacrifice, but, this time, martyrdom finally worked. The AP report seeped into every crack and crevice, right down to the drunken Yabucoa residents running over puppies and hacking up the dogs at Playa Lucia.

I felt devastated, and vindicated. After spending weeks in a post-traumatic haze, this horrible massacre woke me up and forced me to stop feeling sorry for myself.

In early 2008, I received a call to do an interview with *People* magazine. I was thrilled to accept, and didn't flinch when the reporter told me I'd have to pay my own way back to the island. I wanted to keep the momentum the AP article had started going.

It was my first time back since our sudden departure. As I walked the beach with the reporter, dogs poked their noses out of the jungle. I recognized a few of them, but most were new refugees. I walked her around, fed and watered the new dogs, pointed out where things had happened. I showed her where I'd buried twelve hundred of my friends. But it felt as if the place had forgotten me.

We visited the boathouse together. There it sat, still sinking into the sand, still speaking in rusted groans, its dank interior reeking of the same horrible smells. I didn't have to say a word—the reporter understood what I had seen there. The day before, she had interviewed the mayor and numerous other public officials. Luckily, she had seen through their bullshit.

She called her editor from the beach. Surrounded by a pack of mangy, smiling dogs, I heard her say, "He's the real deal. We need to run the story."

After the *People* article ran, a producer from *The Ellen Show* called and asked me to be a guest. I was blown away. I was doing a lot more good here at home than I could ever have done fighting for my dogs, and my life, had I stayed in Puerto Rico.

Appearing on *The Ellen Show* was, for me, the beginning of my real emotional recovery. Ellen herself is a huge animal rights advocate; to have the opportunity to speak with her in front of millions of viewers about the plight of my dogs was everything I could have hoped for. It helped me start believing in the kindness of people again, and, in an odd way, karma. I'd just needed to be patient and accept that the deaths of the twelve hundred dogs I'd buried hadn't been for nothing.

Not only did she help the world learn of the tragedies in Puerto Rico, she donated ten thousand dollars' worth of dog food and supplies from her pet food company, Halo, to help the ongoing rescue and relocation efforts in Puerto Rico.

Soon after this, I founded my own nonprofit organization called the Achates Legacy Rescue Foundation (ALRF), named after my old friend Achates. He'd been my inner strength through the entire Puerto Rican ordeal; his name now represents the heart of my work.

ALRF is based on the belief that, above all, education is the key to saving homeless dogs and cats in our communities and around the world. We promote the creation of educational programs for school systems in target areas, both foreign and domestic, designed to teach adults and children that pets deserve to be treated with dignity and respect.

We also help with the nuts and bolts of survival. Stray dogs and cats living on the beaches, in jungles, and on the streets of target areas throughout the world need food, water, medicine, and treatment in order to survive. You can't rescue a dead pet; you can only bury it.

Additionally, we help support veterinary clinics that provide free spay/neuter services, particularly in Mexico and Puerto Rico. We facilitate rescue and rehabilitation services for abandoned or abused animals, and fund shelters and adoption programs. ALRF also does all it can to help eliminate puppy mills worldwide. This is a fitting tribute to my beloved Achates, and to the thousands of dogs that gave their lives.

There are others continuing the work in Puerto Rico. While the government passed Public Law 154 in 2008, which makes animal abuse and abandonment illegal, it is rarely enforced. Penelope Feliciano, a volunteer with Save a Sato in charge of direct adoptions, works tirelessly to send dogs to shelters or forever homes in the United States. Thanks to a grant from the Millan Foundation, the group was able to spay and neuter a number of shelter animals as well as the pet dogs of people who came to them for help.

As Penelope states, one of the ongoing obstacles in Puerto Rico is the macho culture that feels neutering a male dog will make it homosexual. For many people, dogs are considered a source of income, especially in economically disadvantaged areas. But when puppies don't sell, they are abandoned, and the cycle continues. There is a culture of dogfighting that encourages backyard breeding of pit bulls, which are ultimately left on the streets to die. Given the poor reputation these animals have, and thanks to the violence of this pastime, pit bulls that are lucky enough to be rescued have a hard time finding new homes. It is important to get the word out that pit bulls, like most dogs, are gentle, loving animals, with the right training.

Traer Scott was a nice young woman who had come to Puerto Rico back in 2006 to photograph me with my dogs on the beach for a book she was working on. She and her husband, Jesse, had asked my permission to follow me around during my daily routine with my dogs. She never interfered with my routine while she photographed. In fact, I barely knew she was there.

At the end of that week, she said she'd let me know when her book was published. I received an e-mail from her in 2008 inviting me to a book signing at a Providence area bookstore over Thanksgiving weekend.

I wasn't sure what the book was about, or how I had been portrayed in it. All I knew was that I suddenly felt very vulnerable. I declined the invitation.

"Come run some errands with me," Pam said to me the Saturday after Thanksgiving. "Keep me company."

"Okay. No clothes shopping, though."

"Quiet. Come on."

I wanted to get out of the house anyway, to clear my head.

Twenty minutes later, Pam pulled into the parking lot of a bookstore near our house.

"What are we doing here?"

"Don't worry, it's all good."

As we walked into the store, I saw Traer and Jesse sitting at a table near the entrance. Pam smiled and grabbed my hand.

Traer jumped up, ran over, and hugged me. "Steve! Everyone, this is Stephen McGarva," she said, beaming. "He's the guy from Puerto Rico, the man with the dogs in my book!"

Everyone clapped and welcomed me, almost as if I'd coauthored her book, *Street Dogs*. Traer asked me to sit down and sign books with her, and I was honored to do so. By the end of the evening I had signed dozens of books. No one knew I had never looked inside.

We said our good-byes to Traer and Jesse, then got back in the car, a copy of *Street Dogs* on my lap. I cracked the cover and began turning pages. I immediately recognized my dogs, familiar faces I'd loved for years. Some of them had died defending my life only months after Traer and Jesse had left the island.

"Are you okay?" Pam asked on the ride home.

I didn't answer. I felt like a soldier, the faces of departed friends sitting there in my lap. I started to weep.

Traer had captured the essence of it all. She'd acknowledged me and what I'd done better than anyone else had.

I've been back several times to Dead Dog Beach. It's different now. The approach road has been widened, and the parking lot expanded. The abandoned shipping containers, hiding spots for so many dogs, have been cut up for scrap and carted away, and the area beneath them cleaned. I heard from my friends there that a demolition company had come in with huge machines to tear down the boathouse. The fishermen who plied their trade at the beach had seen it. According to them, when the workers unearthed the dog grave-yard, exposing the bones of the hundreds of dogs I'd buried, a few them got seriously spooked. When I heard the story, I could imagine the backhoes and front-end loaders turning over the soil that held the remains of my lost friends like some apocalyptic vision of hell on earth.

Walking the beach for the last time, I saw only a few furtive dogs, none of which cared to know me. It didn't matter. I'm proud of what I did there in Puerto Rico during those two years.

But I couldn't do it again. I used to live fearlessly and selfishly doing my sports. I climbed at the top of the pack, flew my glider harder than anyone. I was doing things that only a handful of guys in the world were even attempting. I lived like there would be no tomorrow. I never worried about dying. I was fine with it, actually. It was going to happen anyway, so I might as well go out doing something I loved. Now I can take it or leave it. I owe it to Pam, to myself, and, now, to our two beautiful daughters, Freyja and Ella, to make the risks I take more calculated. It's difficult to say how I would have handled things with the dogs if I'd had my daughters at that time. I still take some chances doing rescue work in Mexico and Puerto Rico, but the girls have given me a bigger purpose in life. I know they need me to come home at the end of each day safely. I don't want them to be left without a dad the way I was.

I realize now that I'm no good to any cause if I'm dead.

One of my greatest friends during that two-year period in Puerto Rico was Leo, King of the Beach, who protected me, helped me run the beach, kept order, and lightened my spirit with his sweet, playful heart. I was so pleased when we were able to get him off the beach and into a loving home in upstate New York, in January of 2007. The family who took him owned a nice piece of farm property, allowing Leo to run, play, and explore at will, almost as he'd done on the beach but with the security of a forever family. Their other dog, a yellow Lab named Abby, fell for him right away; they became a loving pack of two.

I always wondered if my old Leo ever thought of me, and of the beach. I liked to think he did, and that he missed me and the camaraderie we shared. But if he didn't, if he'd put it all behind him, then I'd be happy too. I'd envy him his freedom, his clarity of mind, his victory.

While writing this book, I received word of Leo's passing, on June 27, 2011. Over four years of carefree life on a farm, surrounded by those who loved him. What more could one ask for?

No one expects you to move to a foreign country, buy a machete, and start defending strays on the beach. But you can get involved in pet rescue locally, nationally, or internationally by supporting legitimate rescue organizations with your money or time. You can find a local shelter and volunteer once or twice a month, help run fund-raising drives, organize events, or even write letters to your local, state, or federal legislators, particularly with regard to animal abuse legislation. Tell your federal representatives to apply some political pressure on places like Puerto Rico, Mexico, and China where dogs and cats are treated poorly.

Of course, one of the best ways to make a lasting impact is to adopt a homeless pet.

If my book has inspired you to try to help dogs in foreign countries, you can direct your charity toward internationally focused organizations, to help save lives and educate the local people to the plight of unwanted strays. I've listed a few below that I have been personally involved with.

If you decide to volunteer at a local shelter, be prepared to get dirty, and to fall in love with many adorable, needy pets. It is not easy work, but it is rewarding, especially when you play a direct role in saving a dog or cat's life and finding it a home. Nothing compares to the feeling you get when you see a dog or cat doomed to a certain death go home to a loving family.

Below is a list of national and international associations, Web sites, and organizations dedicated to helping rescue and care for pets, both domestic and international. I have also included a short reading list.

ORGANIZATIONS

All Sato Rescue (ASR)

Dedicated to improving the health and reducing the numbers of abandoned dogs in Puerto Rico, ASR rescues, rehabilitates, and finds new homes for "*satos*." Additionally, it strives to address the root causes of overpopulation, abuse, and neglect through initiatives aimed at raising public awareness, facilitating low-cost spay and neuter, and expanding the involvement of government in implementing humane solutions. http://allsatorescue.org

American Society for the Prevention of Cruelty to Animals (ASPCA)

The first of all established humane animal organizations, the well-funded ASPCA provides help and support over a broad spectrum of topics, including rescue, adoption, training, health, and pet counseling. http://www.aspca.org

Cats and Dogs International (CANDI)

An organization that saves the lives of stray cats and dogs in the Caribbean and Mexico through spay, neuter, adoption, and educational programs, CANDI brings tourism businesses together with local animal welfare groups to implement programs that humanely address the issue of cat and dog overpopulation in destination communities. http://www.candiinternational.org

Humane Society International (HSI)

An offshoot of the Humane Society of the United States, HSI focuses its efforts on the suffering of animals in foreign countries. It works with local animal organizations all over the world to provide hands-on care to animals in need and to foster a culture of compassion. http://www.hsi.org

Humane Society of the United States (HSUS)

The largest domestic animal protection organization, HSUS takes an active role in lobbying for animal rights legislation. It participates in national and world-wide rescue efforts, provides sanctuary for needy pets, assists in rehabilitation programs, sets up and runs mobile veterinary clinics, and provides educational programs for animal lovers everywhere. http://www.humanesociety.org

Isla Animals

Isla Animals is dedicated to decreasing the unwanted pet population on Isla Mujeres, Mexico, through ongoing spay/neuter programs, education, vaccinations, and adoption. It offers animal foster care and promotes adoptions in Mexico, the United States, and Canada. Additionally, it educates pet owners about humane animal treatment, care, and responsibility. http://islaanmals.org

Last Chance for Animals (LCA)

Run by actor, author, and animal expert Chris DeRose, LCA has been fighting animal abuse since 1984. It is committed to disseminating truthful information about animal abuse in order to improve the manner in which animals are treated in society. http://www.lcanimal.org/

Save a Gato

A San Juan, Puerto Rico–based group, Save a Gato gives homeless cats on the streets of Old San Juan a chance at a better life. The organization runs a trap-and-neuter program designed to save lives and lower birthrates. It also facilitates adoptions of cats, both in Puerto Rico and to the mainland. http://saveagato.org

Save a Sato Foundation

A Puerto Rico–based volunteer organization dedicated to easing the suffering of Puerto Rico's homeless and abused animals, Save a Sato rescues *satos* from streets and beaches and provides them with medical care, food, shelter, and lots of love. Once rehabilitated, the *satos* are sent to a participating shelter partner for adoption. http://www.saveasato.org

SPCA International

With its focus on international animal welfare issues, the SPCA provides valuable shelter grants, medical assistance, and education and also sponsors targeted rescue efforts worldwide. http://www.spcai.org

Tierra de Animales sanctuary

A refuge for Cancún's forgotten and abandoned street dogs, or "perros callejeros."
http://www.tierradeanimales.org/

World Society for the Protection of Animals (WSPA)

A decades-old organization dedicated to ending animal cruelty worldwide, the WSPA works directly with suffering animals and with local organizations dedicated to helping end animal suffering. Its goal is to get all nations to commit to more animal-friendly practices. http://www.wspa-international.org

RECOMMENDED READING

There are, of course, too many good books to list, but here are just a few that I've found helpful or moving, both in the field of animal rescue and in the basic training of dogs.

Rescue Titles

Street Dogs by Traer Scott (Merrell Publishers, 2007). A lovely collection of ninety black-and-white photographs taken by Traer in 2006 in Puerto Rico, showing *satos* on the streets and beaches. Looking through the book never fails to bring back bittersweet memories for me.

Rescue Matters: How to Find, Foster and Re-home Companion Animals: A Guide for Volunteers and Organizations by Sheila Webster Boneham (Alpine Publishing, 2009). The definitive guide to animal rescue, this book covers all aspects, including starting a rescue group, basic rescue techniques, pet evaluations, and much more. If you want to start your own group or join an established one, read this book.

Rescued: Saving Animals from Disaster by Allen and Linda Anderson (New World Library, 2006). Filled with moving stories of pet rescues in the wake of Hurricane Katrina, this book also provides guidance on proper pet rescue techniques used during times of crisis.

The Lost Dogs: Michael Vick's Dogs and Their Tale of Rescue and Redemption by Jim Gorant (Gotham Publishing, 2010). A gripping story of Michael Vick's dog-fighting operation, and the ensuing efforts to save, rehabilitate, and find homes for the pit bulls he'd doomed to a life of violence and death.

Training and Behavior Books

How to Be Your Dog's Best Friend by the Monks of New Skete (Little, Brown, 2002). This revised version of a classic is both a practical guide to dog training and a philosophical discussion of dog ownership. I like the monks' attitude toward balancing discipline with praise, and their idea that training helps instill a desire to please and perform.

How to Raise the Perfect Dog: Through Puppyhood and Beyond by Cesar Millan and Melissa Jo Peltier (Three Rivers Press, 2010). Aimed at the needs of puppies and young dogs, *How to Raise the Perfect Dog* answers all the most common questions and guides you toward a rewarding rapport with your best canine pal.

The Dog's Mind: Understanding Your Dog's Behavior by Bruce Vogle (Howell Book House, 1992). This is an excellent primer on how dogs perceive the world. Read it if you want to explore how the canine mind works.

ACKNOWLEDGMENTS

To Pamela, my loving and dedicated wife of eighteen years, I love you. You have stood by me through tough times when anyone else would have bailed. You've always supported and encouraged me to pursue my heart's dreams. I know I was tough to live with while living in Puerto Rico and then again while writing this book. It was an emotional and painful journey at times having to relive the memories in order to write the book the way it needed to be written. Through it all, you've remained my constant and helped me to stay the course. Thank you, hon.

To my two beautiful daughters Freyja and Ella, since your arrival in this world, you've managed to provide a piece of my life that I didn't know I was missing. You've breathed a breath of fresh air and new life into me. You've helped me see the little joys in day-to-day living again. Your love and compassion toward animals is inspirational and drives me to be a better person. I love you, my sweeties.

To my oldest daughter Bethany and my only son Curtis. Through all the ups and downs life has thrown our way, my love for you has remained constant. Your compassion and soft-hearted approach to life has always touched me. I love you, kiddos.

To Mum, thank you for always believing in me and helping me to believe in myself. Your encouraging words over the years have allowed me to dream bigger and push myself harder than I thought possible. I love you.

To Barry and Ian, thank you for always being there for me. You've been the best older brothers a rebel like me could have ever asked for. The Mc-Garva brothers forever.

To my closest friend, Yann, thank you, bro!

Nan, Grandpa, Dad, and Blair . . . I love and miss you.

Without the aforementioned, I could never have written this book or done what I did for the dogs at the beach. You took my desperate calls, helped talk me off the ledge of desperation, and kept me from walking away from it all. I'm eternally grateful to each of you for your love and support and for always having my back.